PIZZA
CALIFORNIA STYLE

PIZZA
CALIFORNIA STYLE

More than 80
Fast & Easy Recipes
for Delicious
Gourmet Pizza

N O R M A N   K O L P A S

CB
CONTEMPORARY BOOKS
A TRIBUNE COMPANY

Library of Congress Cataloging-in-Publication Data

Kolpas, Norman.
    Pizza California style : more than 80 fast and easy recipes for
delicious gourmet pizza / Norman Kolpas.
        p.   cm.
    Includes index.
    ISBN 0-8092-4500-0 (P)
0-8092-4312-1 (C)
      1. Pizza.   2. Cookery, American—California style.   3. Quick and
easy cookery.   I. Title.
TX770.P58K65   1989
641.8′24—dc19   88-32460
                                                            CIP

Copyright © 1989 by Norman Kolpas
All rights reserved
Published by Contemporary Books, Inc.
Two Prudential Plaza, Chicago, Illinois 60601-6790
Manufactured in the United States of America
International Standard Book Number: 0-8092-4500-0 (Paper)
                                      0-8092-4312-1 (Cloth)

CONTENTS

PREFACE

California has set the style for the modern pizza.

The state's most creative chefs—particularly those working in and around the major cities of Los Angeles, San Francisco, and San Diego—have taken the rustic Italian flat bread topped with tomato sauce and cheese and elevated it to a signature dish of the New American Cooking.

California-style pizza exhibits many of the characteristics of cuisine on the cutting edge. It's light—based on a thin crust that's eons away from the heavier doughs of traditional pizzas—and baked in small, individual-sized portions. It's fresh—topped with the incomparable produce that the Golden State grows and provides for the entire nation. It's elegant—with even old-fashioned favorites like pepperoni pizza refined to absolute perfection. And it's healthy—reflecting our growing awareness of the benefits of eating vegetables, poultry, and seafood and of dining in moderation.

The pizzas of California are also eclectic and innovative. They pull together strands from Southwestern and Mexican, Japanese, Thai, Chinese, French, Italian, and other cuisines that have taken root in the West. Often, you'll find a number of different cuisines intermingled on the same pizza. You'll notice different sauces beyond the traditional tomato sauce—pestos, pureed peppers, crème fraîche, olive oil, and even no sauce at all.

And, on top of all this, California-style pizza is easy to prepare. The cuisine of California is noted for its casualness and simplicity. Once the easy-to-make basics like dough and sauce have been put together, California-style pizzas are remarkably simple to make with excellent results.

This book offers a comprehensive guide to the California way of making and serving pizza. On the following pages, you'll find information and guidelines for the basics of pizza making: equipment; ingredients; basic recipes; preparation guidelines, including instructions for turning your California pizzas into a related favorite, the calzone (see Index); and serving suggestions. The remainder of the book is divided into four chapters, each offering recipes that feature a specific category of topping—poultry and meats, seafood, vegetables, and cheese.

You'll find pizzas to suit every palate and every occasion, and pizzas that may well offer you new taste experiences. That's part of the spirit of California cuisine. Feel free to join in that spirit yourself and use the recipes as inspiration for devising your own California-style pizzas.

ACKNOWLEDGMENTS

I'd like to thank my team of dedicated tasters, who offered their impartial advice and buoyant enthusiasm: Martha and Henry Cobbold; Peter Goldman; John, Robbie, and Marty Goldman; Hu Goldman and Betty Milius; Molly Lou and Irving Kolpas; Sid, Laurie, Allison, and Jamie Kolpas; Evonne and Joseph Magee; Dave McCombs; Stuart Riskin; and Erica Sagan.

Thanks are also due to Nancy Crossman, who initially suggested the idea for this book, and her colleagues at Contemporary Books. Their unequaled professionalism and trust has been greatly appreciated.

My wife, Katie, was, as always, the most enthusiastic and keenly critical helper and taster of them all, munching through almost every test—making sure that I saved her a slice from those few she missed. This book would have been impossible to write without her support and encouragement.

1
EQUIPMENT AND INGREDIENTS

BASIC PIZZA EQUIPMENT

You don't need much special equipment to make a California-style pizza. In fact, you can get along without any of the equipment I'm about to discuss. But the following items will make it much easier for you to prepare the pizzas, and they'll ensure that you get the best results every time. None of the equipment is particularly expensive, and all of it is readily available in a well-stocked gourmet shop.

Pizza Bricks, Baking Tiles, and Baking Sheets

Professional pizza makers use specially constructed ovens, often of brick, that achieve temperatures several hundred degrees hotter—and substantially drier—than home ovens. The intense, even, dry heat bakes the pizzas quickly, yielding crisp, perfectly browned crusts and golden, bubbling toppings. You can, however, approximate the effect of a professional oven at home by using pizza bricks or baking tiles. After baking the pizzas, be sure to let the tiles or bricks cool completely before handling them.

Pizza bricks. Also known as baking stones, these reasonably priced, commercially produced bricks are made of compacted clay, pressed thin and flat and fired to a temperature of over 2,200°F.

Placed on the middle-to-top shelf of your oven before you preheat it, the brick absorbs moisture and produces an intense, dry heat. Pizzas baked directly on the brick develop evenly browned, wonderfully crisp crusts.

The most widely available pizza bricks seem to be those known as Superstone®, manufactured by Sassafras Enterprises in Evanston, Illinois. Their circular pizza brick measures 13 inches in diameter; the larger, rectangular brick is 12″ × 15″. Both will fit in most home ovens, though the larger one is preferable because you can bake more than one pizza on it at a time. I highly recommend that you use a pizza brick for making your California-style pizzas.

Baking tiles. A traditional home-baking helper, unglazed terra cotta tiles may be placed side-by-side on the oven rack, ready for the pizzas to be placed directly on top. The tiles are more awkward to handle and aren't as durable as commercially made pizza bricks, but they'll give good results.

Baking sheets. In a pinch, you can bake your pizzas on a large baking sheet preheated in the oven. The heavier the sheet, the more heat it will absorb and the better your results will be, but they will be nowhere near as good as pizzas baked on a pizza brick or tiles.

Pizza Paddles or Peels

To transfer your pizzas from the work surface to the oven and then from the oven to your cutting board or serving plate, the best tool is a smooth wooden paddle. Called a "peel" in baker's terminology, it has a tapered edge and should have dimensions at least as big as the pizzas you're baking (in the case of California-style pizzas, at least 8 inches across). The paddle I use at home, widely available at gourmet and kitchen supply stores, has a 14-inch-square blade.

Its tapered edge and smooth surface let you easily slip the paddle under a pizza once you've shaped and topped it. Hold the paddle by its handle and open the oven. A gentle push and shake of your forearm slides the pizza off the paddle onto the preheated pizza brick, tiles, or baking sheet.

When the pizza is done, the paddle can be slipped easily underneath it to remove the pizza from the oven. A pair of wide metal spatulas used together, or a thin, flat, rimless baking sheet, will also do the job, though not as safely or efficiently.

Pizza Cutters

All California-style pizzas may be eaten individually with a knife and fork—and some of them have toppings that make these utensils the best way to eat them—but most of the pizzas in this book are best cut into six slices for eating by hand. There are several tools that will do the job.

Pizza wheels. These are the traditional pizza cutters we've all seen in Italian restaurants—a sturdy wooden or metal handle attached to a rolling wheel with a cutting edge. Virtually all kitchen stores, as well as the kitchenware sections of many supermarkets, carry some form of this utensil.

The most efficient way to use it on a California-style pizza, I find, is to start at the center of the pizza, press down, and roll back and forth to opposite edges of the crust. This tends to leave the toppings as you've arranged them without dragging them across the surface of the pizza.

Chef's knives, Chinese cleavers, and other blades. Another simple way to cut a California-style pizza—particularly a pizza with a thicker or chunkier topping—is with some sort of sharp, heavy kitchen blade longer than the diameter of the pizza and with a somewhat curved edge that allows you to rock the blade when cutting. Large French-style chef's knives, Chinese cleavers, and similar long, heavy, curved blades will do the job well.

Simply place the blade across the pizza, carefully holding it at each end. Press down and gently but firmly rock the blade back and forth across the pizza to cut through. Be sure to take all the precautions you should when handling such a sharp, heavy kitchen tool.

Optional Equipment

There are three pieces of kitchen equipment that aren't crucial to successful results, but make your work so much easier that there's really no sense in doing without them.

Food processors. They're so widespread that they almost seem not worth mentioning. Nevertheless, food processors make kitchen work of any sort so much faster and easier that it's really worth your while to get one. From mixing and kneading doughs to pureeing sauces to shredding cheeses, food processors make California-style pizza making virtually effortless.

There are a number of excellent processor brands on the market. Shop around for one that suits your needs, but be sure it has sufficient capacity to mix up a batch of pizza dough as detailed on the following pages.

Kitchen scales. A kitchen scale makes it incredibly easy to measure ingredients and ensure that you have them in precisely the right proportions—an important factor in getting your pizza toppings just right. It's particularly useful when you split a recipe—making, say, a single pizza instead of the four pizzas for which quantities are given.

Though you can get state-of-the-art electronic scales, all you need is a simple, inexpensive device that will give you precise measurements of relatively small food weights. My favorite is a modern version of the classic counterbalance scale, the Precision Portion Scale made by Cuisinart®. It measures up to 10 ounces, has markings in ¼-ounce increments, and performs with sensitivity and precision.

Oven thermometers. Oven temperatures in home ranges vary widely and may be as much as 50°F or more off the temperature marked on the dial. Though you'll be baking your pizzas at the hottest setting on your home oven, it's a good idea to buy an inexpensive oven thermometer—the kind with a glass tube set in a calibrated metal bracket that can sit on your pizza brick or hang from the oven rack. Use it to set and adjust your oven temperature accurately.

BASIC INGREDIENTS

Apart from the occasional ethnic or gourmet topping for a particular recipe, the ingredients for California-style pizzas are incredibly simple and available in virtually any well-stocked supermarket.

Flours

You'll need just three different flours for making your pizza crusts:

All-purpose flour. Buy any of the well-known commercial or local plain-wrap brands of flour; there's no need for any special bread or cake flours. Feel free to use unbleached flour if you prefer.

Whole-wheat flour. If you want to make wholesome, whole-wheat pizza dough, this is essential. But, as with all-purpose flour, there's no need to go out of your way to buy any special product. Just get whatever whole-wheat flour is available locally.

Semolina flour. I recommend this coarse-textured flour made from hard durum wheat for sprinkling on your work surface when you roll out your pizza dough. It keeps the dough from sticking, makes it easy to slide on and off the pizza paddle, and gives the crust a pleasant, slightly coarse-textured surface. But if you can't get semolina easily, substitute a dusting of regular flour on your work surface; it won't affect your results.

Yeast

Basically, you'll need whatever commercial active dry yeast is available in the baking section of your supermarket. Most such yeasts come packaged in small, ¼-ounce envelopes, one of which is sufficient for a dough recipe that yields four pizzas. If you buy active dry yeast in a can, use 1 level tablespoon in place of one envelope.

For sourdough crusts, you'll have to hunt down a packet of sourdough starter at your local gourmet shop. This consists of special wild yeasts that produce the tangy flavor characteristic of sourdough bread.

Olive Oil

Extra-virgin olive oil—extracted from olives on the first pressing without the use of heat or chemicals—has a rich, fruity flavor that enhances the sauces used on many California-style pizzas. Indeed, you'll find a number of pizzas in which olive oil alone plays the role of sauce.

As a rule, the darker and greener the oil, the more pronounced its flavor. I prefer a dark, fruity oil, but that's a matter of taste and you should seek out one that pleases you. Store the oil in an airtight container, away from light and heat.

Tomatoes

Summer, when tomatoes are at their natural best, is the time to try those recipes that use fresh tomatoes as a topping. I prefer Roma tomatoes because their small, egglike shape gives round, neat slices that make a lovely pattern on top of a pizza.

For pizza sauce, use canned whole or crushed tomatoes. Experiment with those brands available at your local market and find one whose flavor and quality suit your needs. But don't use preseasoned canned tomatoes or tomato sauce, which limit your flexibility in seasoning to your exact tastes.

Herbs

A number of dried and fresh herbs—among them oregano, basil, parsley, chives, thyme, rosemary, and savory—are used to add aromatic variety to California-style pizza toppings. Many supermarkets stock a wide selection of fresh herbs.

The most important fresh herb in this book is basil, which is essential to the Pesto Sauce (see Index) you'll find used in a number of the pizza recipes that follow. If you can't find fresh basil at your local market, try your local garden shop. It's a popular herb for planting in kitchen gardens and window boxes and tends to run rampant—yielding a bountiful supply of the aromatic leaf.

Cheeses

For many people, "pizza" and "cheese" are synonymous. That holds true for California-style pizza too; the only difference is that the range of cheeses has been vastly expanded. Although there are a number of different cheese types, based on how they're made and what goes into them, it's easiest to consider a few simple categories of cheeses:

Grating cheeses. These hard, aged cheeses have a sharp, intense flavor and are usually sprinkled over the sauce as a seasoning. Parmesan is the best known—a rich, tangy cow's milk cheese, aged for more than a year and often two years or more. Also worth keeping on hand are pecorino and Romano—both made from sheep's milk—which are related cheeses with somewhat sharper tastes.

You'll get the best flavor from these cheeses if you buy them whole and grate only as much as you need for a particular recipe. Store the ungrated cheese in the refrigerator, well wrapped in plastic wrap. Keep grated cheese in an airtight container in the refrigerator.

Mozzarellas. Mozzarella is the classic pizza melting cheese, and it plays a major role in California-style pizzas, either on its own or supplementing other cheeses. It is usually spread over the top of the pizza and sometimes underneath large topping ingredients to anchor them in place as it melts.

A well-stocked cheese store offers a lot of choices in mozzarella. The most commonly available is mozzarella made from part-skim milk—a rich-tasting, tangy cheese with good melting properties. Whole-milk mozzarella is also widely available, and though it is excellent in flavor, it may be a touch too rich for some people's tastes.

Fresh mozzarella—often referred to as "buffalo" mozzarella after the buffalo milk traditionally used to make the cheese (cow's milk is the most common source, though), is a mild cheese with a delightful, light, and creamy consistency. It may be found in gourmet shops and Italian delis. Smoked mozzarella acquires a wonderful maple-colored rind and a rich, complex flavor that complements other bold-tasting toppings.

Other melting cheeses. A number of other cheeses with good melting properties are used alone or in combination with each other and mozzarella, adding their taste, texture, and flavor to California-style pizzas. You'll get your best, most dependable selection from a gourmet market or deli.

Among the cheeses you'll find on the following pages are sharp cheddar; tangy, nutlike Swiss cheese; smooth, tangy provolone; mild, sweet Gouda; rich yet subtle fontina; creamy Brie; and all manner of smoked cheeses. Experiment with the cheese available to you locally and add your own favorites to the repertoire.

Specialty cheeses. For the purposes of California-style pizza-making, this wide-ranging category embraces cheeses so distinctive that they dramatically change the character of the pizza they top.

Most remarkable of these are the goat cheeses. Incomparably tangy, rich, and flavorful, these cheeses have become popular ingredients and are representative of cuisine on the cutting edge—not just in California but across the nation and around the world. It's not surprising that they figure so prominently in pizza toppings.

Goat cheese melts to a voluptuously creamy consistency and adds incredible depths of flavor. Fresh goat cheeses have a light taste. Aging develops their distinctive flavor; marinating in olive oil and herbs brings out even greater complexity.

Gourmet markets and delis now stock a wide variety of domestic and imported goat cheeses. Although in some recipes I may suggest specific kinds, the important thing is that you taste several varieties and find one that is pleasing to you.

Blue cheeses give sharp, tangy, creamy flavor to the toppings of some of the pizzas in this book. My favorites—Italian gorgonzola and English stilton—have, by my reckoning, the most distinctive tastes. Feel free to substitute any blue cheese you prefer.

Ricotta is a fresh, smooth cheese made from the whey drained from the curds that go into such cheeses as mozzarella and provolone. It has a mild flavor and, when cooked, a wonderfully light, fluffy texture that enhances the toppings with which it is combined.

Many packaged brands of ricotta are available in well-stocked markets. Some are made of whole milk, some part-skim milk. I prefer the latter, simply because whole-milk ricotta strikes me as a touch too rich.

Two other cheese-related products are used frequently in this book in place of sauces—French-style crème fraîche and Italian mascarpone. Both are made from heavy cream that has been lightly fermented to give a voluptuous thickness to their consistency and a tangy edge to their flavor.

Many gourmet delis and markets now stock one or both of these products. If you can't find them, substitute the heaviest cream that you can find, lightly whipped if necessary, to thicken it.

A Dietary Note on Cheese

Many people are paying special attention to their consumption of cholesterol-rich foods, including dairy products. But a special diet needn't restrict you from eating California-style pizzas.

Today, a number of cheese manufacturers around the country are making special "filled" cheeses from which the butterfat has been removed and replaced by cholesterol-free vegetable fat. You can find filled mozzarella, ricotta, Parmesan, Swiss, cheddar, and virtually any other cheese you can name.

Check your supermarket's cheese case or seek out your local health-food market. If you cannot find such cheeses, ask the manager to order them for you.

A Note on Special and Ethnic Ingredients

California-style pizzas celebrate the ever-growing diversity of foods available to us—not just in California but all over North America. Meat departments and deli cases stock a greater variety of fresh sausages; vegetable departments offer tender baby vegetables, all kinds of onions, elephant garlic, and a wide variety of fresh herbs; specialty and ethnic food aisles are filled with more and more products from Europe and Asia. And adventurous cooks and diners are exploring markets and restaurants in ethnic neighborhoods—Chinese, Japanese, Korean, Latin American. . . .

Throughout this book, you'll find recipes that call for ingredients you may not recognize. Don't be daunted by them. You'll be surprised at how easy they are to find, once you know what to ask for and start to look for them.

2
TIPS FOR PREPARATION AND ENTERTAINING

BASIC PREPARATION STRATEGY

Every pizza recipe in this book includes complete shaping and baking instructions. However, for those who would like some general guidelines—and adventurous cooks who want to try their own original pizza recipes—here are some general instructions.

Preparing the Dough and Sauce

About one hour before you plan to bake and serve the pizzas, begin preparing the dough and the sauce. Note that for sourdough crusts, you'll have to begin preparation up to two days ahead.

Preparing Your Ingredients

Assemble all your topping ingredients, doing the slicing, shredding, marinating, precooking, or other necessary advance preparations.

Preheating the Oven

Put your pizza brick, baking tiles, or a heavy baking sheet in the oven and preheat the oven to 550°F.

Shaping the Pizzas

Place a ball of dough on a work surface sprinkled with semolina. Using the heels of your hands, press down to flatten the dough. Lift and gently pull the dough to stretch it into a circle 8 inches in diameter. With your fingertips, press and shape a ½-inch rim around the crust.

Topping the Pizzas

Spread the sauce over the surface of the pizza up to the rim. Sprinkle any grated cheese over the sauce. Spread a little shredded melting cheese to anchor any large or irregularly shaped topping items. Add your remaining toppings and finish with another layer of melting cheese.

Transferring the Pizzas to the Oven

Slip a pizza paddle under each pizza and transfer it to the baking surface. Slide it from the paddle with a push and a shake of your wrist or forearm.

Baking the Pizzas

Bake the pizzas for 8 to 10 minutes or until their crusts are brown and crisp and their cheese is bubbly and golden. Remove them from the oven with the pizza paddle.

Cutting and Serving the Pizzas

Cut each pizza into six slices with a cutting wheel or curved-edge knife. Any of the pizzas—and particularly those with complex, very chunky, or heavy toppings— may be left uncut, to be eaten with a knife and fork.

ENTERTAINING WITH CALIFORNIA-STYLE PIZZAS

California-style pizzas offer great flexibility for dining and entertaining.

All of the recipes in this book make four single-portion pizzas, sufficient for a lunch or dinner main course. Virtually all of the recipes can easily be halved or quartered, so it also is easy to serve a different pizza to each person, if you wish, or to share a number of different pizzas among you.

Individual slices of the 8-inch pizzas are the ideal size for hors d'oeuvres. You can select several of these recipes, shape and top the pizzas in advance, and bake them in the oven for a hot, fresh cocktail party dish.

Or, you can organize an informal California-style pizza party. Assemble bowls of different sauces and toppings and have balls of pizza dough ready to be shaped. Demonstrate one or two pizzas for your guests, then let them go to work preparing pizzas. You might want to prepare a blackboard or other display offering a few suggested topping combinations from this book to help your less adventurous guests.

3
BASIC CRUSTS, SAUCES, AND TOPPINGS

BASIC RECIPES

These easy-to-prepare recipes for doughs, sauces, and special toppings are the basics of California-style pizza making. All of these basic recipes can be made in advance and stored in the refrigerator. If you like, make several batches and store the dough in the freezer, as described in the following recipes, for future use.

STANDARD PIZZA CRUST

The following recipe produces a thin, golden California-style pizza crust. Parmesan cheese mixed into the dough adds an extra dimension of flavor, and olive oil contributes to its crispness.

1 packet (or 1 tablespoon) active dry yeast	3 tablespoons grated Parmesan cheese
2 teaspoons sugar	1 teaspoon salt
1½ cups lukewarm water	2 tablespoons olive oil
3 cups all-purpose flour	

In a small bowl, dissolve the yeast and 1 teaspoon of the sugar in ½ cup of the lukewarm water. Let it sit until it just begins to foam, 3 to 5 minutes.

Put the flour, Parmesan, salt, and remaining sugar in a food processor fitted with the metal blade. Turning the machine on and off rapidly, pulse several times to blend them. With the machine running, pour in the yeast mixture and oil through the feed tube. Then gradually add enough of the remaining water to form a smooth dough. Continue processing until the dough forms a ball that rides around the work bowl on the blade; the dough at this point will be sufficiently kneaded.

For mixing dough by hand, stir together the dry ingredients in a large bowl and make a well in the center. Add the liquid ingredients and gradually stir from the center outward. When the ingredients are well combined, remove the dough from the bowl and knead it vigorously on a floured work surface for 5 to 7 minutes or until it is smooth and elastic.

Transfer the dough to a large bowl that has been oiled or coated with nonstick spray. Cover the bowl with a damp kitchen towel and let the dough rise for 30 to 45 minutes or until it has doubled in bulk. If it is more convenient, you can let the dough rise in the refrigerator for several hours instead.

Remove the dough from the bowl and cut it into four equal portions weighing about 6 ounces each, one per pizza. The dough is ready to shape and bake.

To freeze the dough, wrap each ball securely in plastic wrap and place in the freezer. The dough will keep well for several weeks. Defrost it at room temperature for 2 to 3 hours, or all day in the refrigerator, before making the pizzas.

Makes about 1½ pounds dough; serves 4

WHOLE-WHEAT PIZZA CRUST

This honey-enriched whole-wheat dough has a full, earthy flavor and a texture that suits it well to more robust pizzas. Only a third of the flour used, though, is whole wheat; the all-purpose flour makes the dough more manageable and results in a lighter, crisper crust.

1 package (or 1 tablespoon) active dry yeast	2 cups all-purpose flour
2 teaspoons honey	1 cup whole-wheat flour
1½ cups lukewarm water	1 teaspoon salt
	2 tablespoons corn oil

In a small bowl, dissolve the yeast and 1 teaspoon of the honey in ½ cup of the lukewarm water. Let it sit until it just begins to foam, 3 to 5 minutes.

Put the all-purpose and whole-wheat flours and the salt in a food processor fitted with the metal blade. Turning the machine on and off rapidly, pulse several times to blend them. With the machine running, pour in the yeast mixture, remaining honey, and oil through the feed tube. Then gradually add enough of the remaining water to form a smooth dough. Continue processing until the dough forms a ball that rides around the work bowl on the blade; the dough at this point will be sufficiently kneaded.

For mixing dough by hand, stir together the dry ingredients in a large bowl and make a well in the center. Add the liquid ingredients and gradually stir from the center outwards. When the ingredients are well combined remove the dough from the bowl and knead it vigorously on a floured work surface for 5 to 7 minutes or until it is smooth and elastic.

Transfer the dough to a large bowl that has been oiled or coated with nonstick spray. Cover the bowl with a damp kitchen towel and let the dough rise for 30 to 45 minutes or until it has doubled in bulk. If it is more convenient, you can let the dough rise in the refrigerator for several hours instead.

Remove the dough from the bowl and cut it into four equal portions weighing about 6 ounces each, one for each pizza. The dough is ready to shape and bake.

To freeze the dough, wrap each ball securely in plastic wrap and place in the freezer. The dough will keep well for several weeks. Defrost it at room temperature for 2 to 3 hours, or all day in the refrigerator, before making the pizzas.

Makes about 1½ pounds dough; serves 4

SOURDOUGH PIZZA CRUST

Sourdough gives an authentically tangy old-California flavor to modern California-style pizzas. Buy commercial sourdough starter from your local gourmet food shop or supermarket.

You have to plan to make this dough in advance because it takes the starter 1½ to 2 days to develop its characteristic flavor.

SOURDOUGH STARTER
1 (½-ounce) packet
    sourdough starter
1 cup all-purpose flour
¾ cup lukewarm water

SOURDOUGH PIZZA DOUGH
½ packet (or ½ tablespoon)
    active dry yeast
½ teaspoon sugar
1 cup lukewarm water
2 cups all-purpose flour
1 teaspoon salt
1 tablespoon olive oil

Prepare the Sourdough Starter 2 days before you plan to make the pizzas. In a large mixing bowl, stir together the contents of the starter packet with the flour. Then stir in the water until smooth. Cover the bowl with plastic wrap and leave it in a warm spot, away from drafts, for 1½ to 2 days. It will develop bubbles and give off a sour aroma.

Then transfer the starter mixture, still covered, to the refrigerator, where it will remain dormant until use.

Remove the starter mixture from the refrigerator 1 to 2 hours before preparing the pizza dough; let it come to room temperature.

In a small bowl, dissolve the dry yeast and the sugar in ½ cup of the lukewarm water. Let it sit until it just begins to foam, 3 to 5 minutes.

Put the flour and salt in a food processor fitted with the metal blade. Turning the machine on and off rapidly, pulse several times to blend. With the machine running, pour in the Sourdough Starter, yeast mixture, and oil through the feed tube. Then gradually add just enough of the remaining water to form a smooth dough.

Continue processing until the dough forms a ball that rides around the work bowl on the blade; the dough at this point will be sufficiently kneaded.

For mixing dough by hand, stir together the dry ingredients in a large bowl and make a well in the center. Add the liquid ingredients and gradually stir from the center outwards. When the ingredients are well combined, remove the dough from the bowl and knead it vigorously on a floured work surface for 5 to 7 minutes or until it is smooth and elastic.

Transfer the dough to a large bowl that has been oiled or coated with nonstick spray. Cover the bowl with a damp kitchen towel and let the dough rise for 30 to 45 minutes or until it has doubled in bulk. If it is more convenient, you can let the dough rise in the refrigerator for several hours instead.

Remove the dough from the bowl and cut it into four equal portions weighing about 6 ounces each, one for each pizza. The dough is ready to shape and bake.

To freeze the dough, wrap each ball securely in plastic wrap and place in the freezer. The dough will keep well for several weeks. Defrost it at room temperature for 2 to 3 hours, or all day in the refrigerator, before making the pizzas.

Makes about 1½ pounds dough; serves 4

PIZZA DOUGH SUBSTITUTES

While the preceding pizza dough recipes are quick and easy to make, don't forget that most supermarkets now stock some form of ready-to-bake bread dough in the freezer case, which will save you additional preparation time. Indeed, you may find several different kinds of dough. Just buy enough to give you four (6-ounce) balls of dough per recipe.

A new product called Boboli® offers yet another option. These packaged, pizza-shaped bread rounds come already baked; just top and heat them in a 450°F–500°F oven until the cheese melts and the bread crisps. Individual Bobolis, however, come in a 6-inch rather than an 8-inch size, so you'll have to halve the topping ingredients in any particular recipe to get the right amounts for the smaller surface areas. (I know a pizza 6 inches in diameter doesn't seem half as big as an 8-incher, but it does work out to be about half if you apply the old high-school geometry formula to figure the area of a circle.)

TOMATO SAUCE

The quantities below will make enough for two separate pizza recipes—eight pizzas in all. If you're making only four pizzas—that is, one recipe—you can either halve the ingredients or store the remainder in the refrigerator for up to a week or in an airtight container in the freezer for several months.

If absolutely necessary, substitute the best seasoned commercial tomato sauce—labeled Pizza Sauce or Marinara Sauce—you can find.

2 tablespoons olive oil
3 medium garlic cloves, finely chopped
¼ medium-sized brown-skinned onion, finely chopped
1 (28-ounce) can crushed tomatoes

1 tablespoon sugar
¾ teaspoon dried marjoram
¾ teaspoon salt
6 fresh basil leaves, finely chopped (or 1 tablespoon dried basil)

In a medium saucepan, heat the olive oil over medium heat. Add the garlic and onion and sauté until transparent, 3 to 5 minutes.

Add the remaining ingredients. Reduce the heat slightly and simmer, stirring frequently, until thick, 25 to 30 minutes.

Makes about 2 cups

BARBECUE SAUCE

The quantities below will make enough for two separate pizza recipes—eight pizzas in all. If you're making only four pizzas—that is, one recipe—you can either halve the ingredients or store the remainder in the refrigerator for up to a week or in an airtight container in the freezer for several months.

If absolutely necessary, substitute the best-quality store-bought barbecue sauce you can find.

2 tablespoons corn oil
2 medium garlic cloves, finely chopped
¼ medium-sized brown-skinned onion, finely chopped
1 (16-ounce) can tomato puree
3 tablespoons dark brown sugar

2 tablespoons molasses
2 tablespoons red wine vinegar
¾ teaspoon salt
½ teaspoon liquid natural hickory seasoning ("Liquid Smoke")
½ teaspoon crushed red pepper flakes
½ teaspoon dried oregano

In a medium saucepan, heat the oil over medium heat. Add the garlic and onion and sauté until transparent, 3 to 5 minutes.

Add the remaining ingredients. Reduce the heat slightly and simmer, stirring frequently, until thick, about 10 minutes.

Makes about 2 cups

PESTO SAUCE

This authentic Northern Italian sauce is made with basil. Because pesto darkens if left in contact with air or stored too long, I have given quantities sufficient for just one recipe—that is, four pizzas. However, the recipe is easily doubled or tripled.

A number of commercial pesto sauces are available. But read the labels carefully—some substitute parsley or spinach for part of the basil, resulting in a less aromatic, less flavorful sauce.

1¼ cups fresh basil leaves
½ cup grated Parmesan cheese
½ cup olive oil
3 medium garlic cloves, peeled

⅓ cup pine nuts, toasted until golden in a 450°F oven, about 10 minutes (watch carefully to avoid burning them)

Put all the ingredients into a food processor fitted with the metal blade. Turning the machine on and off rapidly, pulse the ingredients several times until coarsely chopped. Scrape down the work bowl. Then process continuously until the sauce is smooth.

Makes about 1 cup

ROASTED GARLIC CLOVES

Cloves of roasted garlic are a popular topping for California-style pizzas. Roasting takes the sharp edge off the flavor of garlic, yielding wonderfully aromatic cloves with just a hint of sweetness.

To roast garlic, loosely but securely wrap one or more whole heads—the individual cloves left clustered with their peels intact—in heavy-duty aluminum foil or a double thickness of regular foil. Roast the garlic heads in a 425°F oven for about an hour, until the individual cloves are so soft that the tip of a small sharp knife can pierce a clove with no resistance. (Your kitchen—and possibly your entire home—will fill with the smell of roasting garlic.)

Leave the foil packages on the kitchen counter until the garlic is cool enough to handle. Fill a bowl with olive oil.

Carefully separate the cloves—you may need a small, sharp knife to cut away the root end of the garlic head. With your fingers, squeeze the cloves one-by-one into the oil. Most of the cloves will emerge from their skins in a single, soft piece; some will run out in a thin stream.

Make sure that all the roasted garlic is covered with the oil. Cover the bowl with plastic wrap and store in the refrigerator.

ROASTED PEPPERS

Roasting develops the inherent sweetness of bell peppers. Once roasted, peeled, and seeded, the peppers are easily torn into strips, to be strewn on top of pizzas.

To roast peppers, place them on a baking sheet in a 500°F oven. Roast until their skins are evenly blistered and browned, about 25 minutes, turning them two or three times so they roast evenly. Remove them from the oven and cover them with a kitchen towel.

When the peppers are cool enough to handle, pull out their stems; peel away their blackened skins; open the peppers up; and remove their seeds, using a teaspoon to pick up any stray ones.

Place roasted peppers in a bowl, submerge them in olive oil, and cover the bowl with plastic wrap before storing it in the refrigerator.

A NOTE ON CALZONES

An offshoot of California-style pizza's popularity is the resurgence of the traditional Italian pizza turnover—the calzone. The word means "slipper," a fanciful description of the turnover's plump shape.

California-style calzones are incredibly easy to make. Choose any pizza recipe with substantial yet compact toppings that aren't likely to fall out of the calzone or hinder you from cutting it neatly. I've indicated in the individual recipe introductions if a particular pizza is appropriate for adapting to a calzone.

To make a calzone, assemble the same ingredients in the same quantities listed for the pizzas. Preheat the oven—with a pizza brick, baking tiles, or baking sheet—to 550°F.

Shape the balls of pizza dough as you would for a pizza, flattening and stretching them on a work surface sprinkled with semolina, until they form circles 8 inches in diameter with raised rims.

Spread the sauce over the entire surface of the dough up to the rim. But neatly arrange the other topping ingredients on only the half of the dough nearest you.

Then lift the farthest edge of the dough and fold it toward you over the filling, neatly aligning the edges of the dough to form a semicircular turnover. With your thumbs and forefingers, press and crimp the edges together to secure the filling.

Carefully slide a pizza paddle under the calzones one at a time and transfer them to the oven. With a slight push, slide each calzone off the paddle onto the baking surface. Bake for 8 to 10 minutes or until the dough is browned and crisp.

Cut the calzone into three or four wedges with a pizza wheel or curved edge knife, or serve it whole, to be eaten with a knife and fork.

4
POULTRY AND MEAT TOPPINGS

BARBECUED CHICKEN

GRILLED CHICKEN WITH RED ONION, BLACK OLIVES, AND PESTO

CHICKEN TERIYAKI

INDONESIAN CHICKEN

GROUND SPICY CHICKEN WITH SPINACH AND ROASTED GARLIC

CHINESE-STYLE DUCK

DUCK SAUSAGE WITH SWEET RED PEPPERS AND SUN-DRIED TOMATOES

TURKEY SAUSAGE AND GREEN PEPPERS

REUBEN

BEEF FAJITAS WITH FRESH MOZZARELLA AND GUACAMOLE

GROUND BEEF, BLACK OLIVES, EGG, AND ONION

SMOKED BEEF, SUN-DRIED TOMATOES, AND PECORINO WITH PEPPER
CANADIAN BACON, EGG, AND CHEDDAR
PROSCIUTTO AND FONTINA WITH MARINATED OLIVES
CLASSIC PEPPERONI
HOT ITALIAN SAUSAGE, SWEET RED PEPPERS, AND MAUI ONIONS
ANDOUILLE SAUSAGE WITH VIDALIA ONIONS, CORN, AND GREEN PEPPER
VEAL MEATBALL WITH ENOKI MUSHROOMS, HERBS, AND RICOTTA
WHITE VEAL SAUSAGE WITH MUSTARD, YELLOW BELL PEPPERS, AND BRIE
MARINATED LAMB WITH BLACK OLIVES, ROASTED PEPPERS, AND FETA
GROUND LAMB WITH EGGPLANT, PESTO, AND PINE NUTS

BARBECUED CHICKEN

In some form or another, you'll find a barbecued chicken pizza on the menu of virtually every restaurant that serves California-style pizzas. This one, with its red onion, green flecks of cilantro, and yellow bell pepper strips, is a wonderfully colorful version. Substitute green or red bell peppers, if you like.

You may find it easier to eat this pizza with a knife and fork.

1½ cups Barbecue Sauce (recipe on page 19)

2 boned and skinned chicken breasts (about 1 pound total), trimmed of fat and halved to make four half-breasts

4 (6-ounce) balls pizza dough; use a Standard, Whole-Wheat, or Sourdough Pizza Crust (recipes on pages 14–16)

¼ cup chopped fresh cilantro leaves

½ pound provolone cheese, shredded

1½ cups thinly sliced red onion

1 medium yellow bell pepper, stemmed, quartered, seeded, and cut crosswise into ¼-inch-wide strips

Place a pizza brick, baking tiles, or a baking sheet in the oven and preheat the oven to 550°F.

Put ½ cup of the Barbecue Sauce in a bowl, add the chicken breasts, and turn to coat them evenly. Marinate at room temperature for 15 to 30 minutes, turning them two or three times.

Preheat the grill or broiler until very hot, with the cooking surface close to the heat. Grill or broil the chicken breasts about 1 minute per side, until they are seared but still pink. With a sharp knife held at a 45-degree angle crosswise, carve the chicken into ¼-inch-thick slices.

Place a ball of dough on a work surface sprinkled with semolina. Using the heels of your hands, press down to flatten the dough. Lift and gently pull the dough to stretch it into a circle 8 inches in diameter. With your fingertips, press and shape a ½-inch rim around the crust. Repeat with remaining balls of dough. Spread ¼ cup of the remaining sauce on each piece of dough up to the rim. Sprinkle the cilantro on each. Using about a quarter of the cheese, sprinkle an equal portion of it on each pizza.

Arrange the onions and peppers on top of each pizza, then place the chicken slices on top. Spread an equal portion of the remaining cheese over each pizza.

Carefully slide a pizza paddle under the pizzas, one at a time, and transfer them to the oven; with a slight push, slide each pizza off the paddle onto the baking surface. Bake the pizzas for 8 to 10 minutes or until the dough is browned and crisp and the cheese is golden and bubbly.

Serves 4

GRILLED CHICKEN WITH RED ONION, BLACK OLIVES, AND PESTO

This is a classic example of how a few really simple ingredients can be put together to make a memorable combination.

¼ cup olive oil
2 tablespoons lemon juice
1 tablespoon dried oregano
2 boned and skinned chicken breasts (about 1 pound total), trimmed of fat and halved to make four half-breasts
Salt and freshly ground black pepper
4 (6-ounce) balls pizza dough; use a Sourdough or Whole-Wheat Pizza Crust (recipes on pages 15–16)

1 cup Pesto Sauce (recipe on page 20)
½ cup grated Parmesan cheese
48 marinated black olives, halved and pitted
¾ pound mozzarella cheese, shredded
1 large red onion, thinly sliced

Place a pizza brick, baking tiles, or a baking sheet in the oven and preheat the oven to 550°F.

Put the olive oil and lemon juice in a bowl, crumble in the oregano, add the chicken breasts, and turn to coat them evenly. Marinate at room temperature for 15 to 30 minutes, turning them two or three times.

Preheat the grill or broiler until very hot, with the cooking surface close to the heat. Sprinkle the chicken breasts with salt and pepper and grill or broil them about 1 minute per side, until they are seared but still pink. With a sharp knife held at a 45-degree angle, carve the chicken crosswise into ¼-inch-thick slices.

Place a ball of dough on a work surface sprinkled with semolina. Using the heels of your hands, press down to flatten the dough. Lift and gently pull the dough to stretch it into a circle 8 inches in diameter. With your fingertips, press and shape a ½-inch rim around the crust. Repeat with remaining balls of dough.

Spread ¼ cup of the sauce on each piece of dough up to the rim. Sprinkle the Parmesan equally on each pizza and dot with the black olive halves. Using about one-third of the mozzarella, sprinkle an equal portion of it on each pizza.

Arrange the chicken slices on top of each pizza and spread the onion slices over the chicken. Top with the remaining mozzarella.

Carefully slide a pizza paddle under the pizzas, one at a time, and transfer them to the oven; with a slight push, slide each pizza off the paddle onto the baking surface. Bake the pizzas for 8 to 10 minutes or until the dough is browned and crisp and the cheese is golden and bubbly.

Serves 4

CHICKEN TERIYAKI

The Japanese influence is strong in California and freely interpreted, as this fanciful creation bears witness. Use the best commercially prepared sauces you can find in the Asian food section of your supermarket.

¼ cup teriyaki sauce

2 boned and skinned chicken breasts (about 1 pound total), trimmed of fat and halved to make 4 half-breasts

4 (6-ounce) balls pizza dough; use a Standard Pizza Crust (recipe on page 14)

1 cup plum sauce

3 tablespoons grated orange zest

¾ pound mozzarella cheese, shredded

5 fresh or canned and drained pineapple rings, about ¼-inch thick (about 6 ounces fruit), cut into ¼-inch-wide wedges

2 medium red bell peppers, stemmed, quartered, seeded, and cut crosswise into ¼-inch-wide strips

Place a pizza brick, baking tiles, or a baking sheet in the oven and preheat the oven to 550°F.

Put the teriyaki sauce in a bowl, add the chicken breasts and turn to coat them evenly. Marinate at room temperature for 15 to 30 minutes, turning them two or three times.

Preheat the grill or broiler until very hot, with the cooking surface close to the heat. Grill or broil the chicken breasts about 1 minute per side, until they are seared but still pink. With a sharp knife held at a 45-degree angle, carve the chicken crosswise into ¼-inch-thick slices.

Place a ball of dough on a work surface sprinkled with semolina. Using the heels of your hands, press down to flatten the dough. Lift and gently pull the dough to stretch it into a circle 8 inches in diameter. With your fingertips, press and shape a ½-inch rim around the crust. Repeat with remaining balls of dough.

Spread ¼ cup of plum sauce on each piece of dough up to the rim. Sprinkle the orange zest on each. Using one-third of the mozzarella, sprinkle an equal portion of it on each pizza.

Arrange the chicken slices on top of each pizza and distribute the pineapple wedges and pepper strips. Top the pizzas with the remaining mozzarella.

Carefully slide a pizza paddle under the pizzas, one at a time, and transfer them to the oven; with a slight push, slide each pizza off the paddle onto the baking surface. Bake the pizzas for 8 to 10 minutes or until the dough is browned and crisp and the cheese is golden and bubbly.

Serves 4

INDONESIAN CHICKEN

This pizza won its highest compliment from my wife, Katie, who looked disgusted when I described it to her but helped herself to a second slice after her first hesitant bite. The toppings are typical ingredients in Indonesian cooking, a marvelous cuisine I was introduced to by my friend Copeland Marks, author of The Indonesian Kitchen.

¼ cup plus 2 teaspoons hot chili sesame oil

¼ cup plus 1 teaspoon tamari sauce

2 boned and skinned chicken breasts (about 1 pound total), trimmed of fat and halved to make 4 half-breasts

¾ cup peanut butter

4 teaspoons dark brown sugar

4 (6-ounce) balls pizza dough; use a Standard Pizza Crust (recipe on page 14)

6 tablespoons shredded coconut

6 tablespoons roasted, unsalted peanut halves

6 tablespoons chopped fresh scallion

6 tablespoons shredded carrot

3 tablespoons coarsely chopped cilantro leaves

½ pound port salut cheese

6 ounces mozzarella cheese, shredded

Place a pizza brick, baking tiles, or a baking sheet in the oven and preheat the oven to 550°F.

In a bowl, stir together ¼ cup each of the hot chili sesame oil and tamari sauce. Add the chicken breasts and turn to coat them evenly. Marinate at room temperature for 15 to 30 minutes, turning them two or three times.

Preheat the grill or broiler until very hot, with the cooking surface close to the heat. Grill or broil the chicken breasts about 1 minute per side, until they are seared but still pink. With a sharp knife held at a 45-degree angle, carve the chicken crosswise into ¼-inch-thick slices.

In another bowl, stir together the peanut butter and dark brown sugar with the remaining chili sesame oil and tamari sauce.

Place a ball of dough on a work surface sprinkled with semolina. Using the heels of your hands, press down to flatten the dough. Lift and gently pull the

dough to stretch it into a circle 8 inches in diameter. With your fingertips, press and shape a ½-inch rim around the crust. Repeat with remaining balls of dough. Spread one quarter of the sauce on each piece of dough up to the rim.

Line a baking sheet with aluminum foil and sprinkle the coconut evenly over the foil. Put the sheet in the preheated oven and toast the coconut until golden, no more than 30 seconds; watch carefully so the coconut doesn't burn.

Sprinkle the toasted coconut equally on each pizza. Then sprinkle the peanuts, scallions, and carrot on each crust.

Arrange the chicken slices on top of each pizza and scatter the cilantro over the pizzas. Dot the chicken with the port salut cheese and then distribute the mozzarella evenly over each pizza.

Carefully slide a pizza paddle under the pizzas, one at a time, and transfer them to the oven; with a slight push, slide each pizza off the paddle onto the baking surface. Bake the pizzas for 8 to 10 minutes or until the dough is browned and crisp and the cheese is golden and bubbly.

Serves 4

GROUND SPICY CHICKEN WITH
SPINACH AND ROASTED GARLIC

There's a strong Mexican influence in the chicken mixture that tops this colorful, healthful pizza. Roasted garlic cloves add mellow and sweet flavors. If you prefer, substitute half the amount of fresh garlic, finely chopped and scattered over the sauce.

Take special care when handling hot chilies such as jalapeños not to touch your eyes and to wash your hands well after working with the chilies.

May also be made as a calzone (see page 23).

¼ cup olive oil (preferably from Roasted Garlic Cloves)

1 jalapeño chili, stemmed, seeded, and finely chopped

1 medium onion, finely chopped

1 teaspoon ground cumin

1 teaspoon ground coriander

1 teaspoon ground chili powder

1 pound ground chicken breast

½ teaspoon salt

4 (6-ounce) balls pizza dough; use a Standard, Sourdough, or Whole-Wheat Pizza Crust (recipes on pages 14, 15 and 16)

1 cup Tomato Sauce (recipe on page 18)

32 medium Roasted Garlic Cloves (recipe on page 21)

¾ pound mozzarella cheese, shredded

16 large spinach leaves, thoroughly washed, patted dry, stemmed, ribbed, and cut crosswise into ¼-inch-wide strips

Place a pizza brick, baking tiles, or a baking sheet in the oven and preheat the oven to 550°F.

In a large saucepan, heat the oil over medium heat. Add the chili and onion and sauté until soft, 2 to 3 minutes. Add the spices and sauté about 30 seconds more. Add the chicken and salt and sauté until cooked through, 3 to 5 minutes, stirring frequently with a wooden spoon to break up the chicken. Carefully pour off the excess fat from the pan.

Place a ball of dough on a work surface sprinkled with semolina. Using the heels of your hands, press down to flatten the dough. Lift and gently pull the

dough to stretch it into a circle 8 inches in diameter. With your fingertips, press and shape a ½-inch rim around the crust. Repeat with remaining balls of dough.

Spread ¼ cup of the sauce on each piece of dough up to the rim. Distribute the Roasted Garlic Cloves over the sauce on each pizza, pressing down gently to spread them out. Using about a quarter of the cheese, sprinkle it equally on each pizza.

Distribute the chicken mixture evenly over the pizzas. Scatter the spinach over the chicken on each. Then top pizzas with the remaining cheese.

Carefully slide a pizza paddle under the pizzas, one at a time, and transfer them to the oven; with a slight push, slide each pizza off the paddle onto the baking surface. Bake the pizzas for 8 to 10 minutes or until the dough is browned and crisp and the cheese is golden and bubbly.

Serves 4

CHINESE-STYLE DUCK

Think of this as Peking duck on a pizza, without the crisp duck skin—which I prefer to omit for the obvious savings in fat and calories. You can get duck breasts from most butchers, though you may have to order them in advance.

Buy the best-quality prepared Chinese sauces you can find; they're available in the Asian food sections of most good-sized supermarkets.

2 tablespoons teriyaki sauce
2 tablespoons sesame oil
2 boned and skinned duck breasts (about 1 pound total) trimmed of fat and halved to make 4 half-breasts
4 (6-ounce) balls pizza dough; use a Standard Pizza Crust (recipe on page 14)

½ cup hoisin sauce
5 tablespoons black bean sauce
¼ cup chopped scallion
6 ounces fresh shiitake mushrooms, stemmed and cut crosswise into ¼-inch-wide pieces
10 ounces mozzarella cheese, shredded

Place a pizza brick, baking tiles, or a baking sheet in the oven and preheat the oven to 550°F.

In a bowl, stir together the teriyaki sauce and sesame oil. Add the duck breasts and turn them to coat evenly. Marinate at room temperature for 15 to 30 minutes, turning them two or three times.

Preheat the grill or broiler until very hot, with the cooking surface close to the heat. Grill or broil the duck breasts about 1½ minutes per side, until they are seared but still pink. With a sharp knife held at a 45-degree angle, carve the duck crosswise into ¼-inch-thick slices.

Place a ball of dough on a work surface sprinkled with semolina. Using the heels of your hands, press down to flatten the dough. Lift and gently pull the dough to stretch it into a circle 8 inches in diameter. With your fingertips, press and shape a ½-inch rim around the crust. Repeat with remaining balls of dough.

Stir together the hoisin and black bean sauces and spread one quarter on each piece of dough up to the rim. Sprinkle the scallion over the sauce, then distribute the shiitake slices. Using half of the cheese, distribute it evenly on each pizza.

Place the duck slices on top of the mozzarella on each pizza. Then spread the remaining cheese on top.

Carefully slide a pizza paddle under the pizzas, one at a time, and transfer them to the oven; with a slight push, slide each pizza off the paddle onto the baking surface. Bake the pizzas for 8 to 10 minutes or until the dough is browned and crisp and the cheese is golden and bubbly.

Serves 4

DUCK SAUSAGE WITH SWEET RED PEPPERS AND SUN-DRIED TOMATOES

Many gourmet butcher shops now carry duck sausage. If it's not available in your area, substitute turkey sausage or even sweet Italian sausage.
May also be made as a calzone (see page 23).

4 fresh duck sausages, 3½ to 4 ounces each
4 (6-ounce) balls pizza dough; use a Sourdough or Standard Pizza Crust (recipes on pages 16 and 14)
1 cup Tomato Sauce (recipe on page 18)

36 sun-dried tomato pieces
4 medium red bell peppers, roasted (recipe on page 22) and torn into ¼-inch-wide strips
¼ pound provolone cheese, shredded
6 ounces mozzarella cheese, shredded

Place a pizza brick, baking tiles, or a baking sheet in the oven and preheat the oven to 550°F.

Preheat the grill or broiler until very hot, with the cooking surface close to the heat.

Put the sausages in a saucepan and add enough cold water to cover them. Cover the pan and bring the water to a boil over moderate heat. As soon as the water boils, drain the sausages.

With a fork, puncture each sausage in a few places and transfer to the grill or broiler. Cook the sausages for 1½ to 2 minutes per side, until their skins are just browned.

Place a ball of dough on a work surface sprinkled with semolina. Using the heels of your hands, press down to flatten the dough. Lift and gently pull the dough to stretch it into a circle 8 inches in diameter. With your fingertips, press and shape a ½-inch rim around the crust. Repeat with remaining balls of dough.

Spread ¼ cup of the sauce on each piece of dough up to the rim. Distribute the sun-dried tomatoes and pepper strips on top of the sauce. Top each with one quarter of the provolone.

Cut the sausages with a sharp knife held at a 45-degree angle into ¼- to ½-inch-thick slices. Distribute the slices evenly on each pizza. Spread one quarter of the mozzarella on top of each.

Carefully slide a pizza paddle under the pizzas, one at a time, and transfer them to the oven; with a slight push, slide each pizza off the paddle onto the baking surface. Bake the pizzas for 8 to 10 minutes or until the dough is browned and crisp and the cheese is golden and bubbly.

Serves 4

On preceding page:
Grilled Chicken with Red Onion, Black Olives, and Pesto (page 28)
At left:
Chinese-Style Duck (page 36)

TURKEY SAUSAGE AND GREEN PEPPERS

Many butchers and delis now make excellent turkey sausage—both dinner and breakfast varieties—that have all the flavor of but less fat and calories than conventional pork sausages.

May also be made as a calzone (see page 23).

4 (6-ounce) balls pizza dough; use a Standard, Whole-Wheat, or Sourdough Pizza Crust (recipes on pages 14–16)

1 cup Tomato Sauce (recipe on page 18)

½ cup grated Parmesan cheese

¾ pound fresh turkey sausage, casings slit and removed

1 medium green bell pepper, stemmed, quartered, seeded, and cut crosswise into ¼-inch-wide strips

6 ounces provolone cheese, shredded

¼ pound mozzarella cheese, shredded

Place a pizza brick, baking tiles, or a baking sheet in the oven and preheat the oven to 550°F.

Place a ball of dough on a work surface sprinkled with semolina. Using the heels of your hands, press down to flatten the dough. Lift and gently pull the dough to stretch it into a circle 8 inches in diameter. With your fingertips, press and shape a ½-inch rim around the crust. Repeat with remaining balls of dough. Spread ¼ cup of the sauce on each piece of dough up to the rim. Sprinkle the Parmesan equally on each pizza.

With your fingertips, pinch off small pieces of the sausage meat and dot them on top of the pizzas. Scatter the pepper strips over the pizzas and top with the provolone and mozzarella.

Carefully slide a pizza paddle under the pizzas, one at a time, and transfer them to the oven; with a slight push, slide each pizza off the paddle onto the baking surface. Bake the pizzas for 8 to 10 minutes or until the dough is browned and crisp and the cheese is golden and bubbly.

Serves 4

REUBEN

Based on the deli classic, this pizza is a delightfully elegant surprise.
May also be made as a calzone (see page 23).

4 (6-ounce) balls pizza dough; use a Standard or Sourdough Pizza Crust (recipes on pages 14 and 16)

½ cup grainy Dijon-style mustard

½ cup crème fraîche or heavy cream

1½ cups thoroughly drained sauerkraut

6 ounces kosher dill pickles, quartered lengthwise, and cut crosswise into ¼-inch-thick pieces

¾ pound Swiss cheese, shredded

10 ounces lean corned beef, thinly sliced

Place a pizza brick, baking tiles, or a baking sheet in the oven and preheat the oven to 550°F.

Place a ball of dough on a work surface sprinkled with semolina. Using the heels of your hands, press down to flatten the dough. Lift and gently pull the dough to stretch it into a circle 8 inches in diameter. With your fingertips, press and shape a ½-inch rim around the crust. Repeat with remaining balls of dough. Stir together the mustard and crème fraîche or cream and spread one quarter of the mixture on each piece of dough up to the rim.

Distribute the sauerkraut evenly over the sauce on each pizza and scatter the pickle pieces on top. Scatter about a quarter of the cheese evenly over the pizzas. Drape the corned beef over the other ingredients, then distribute the remaining cheese over the tops of the pizzas.

Carefully slide a pizza paddle under the pizzas, one at a time, and transfer them to the oven; with a slight push, slide each pizza off the paddle onto the baking surface. Bake the pizzas for 8 to 10 minutes or until the dough is browned and crisp and the cheese is golden and bubbly.

Serves 4

BEEF FAJITAS WITH FRESH MOZZARELLA AND GUACAMOLE

California has done its share to popularize Mexican fajitas—grilled strips of meat, peppers, and onion. Although the meat and vegetables ordinarily are wrapped in hot tortillas, they make an excellent pizza topping. Take special care when handling hot chilies such as jalapeños not to touch your eyes and to wash your hands well after working with the chilies.

¾ pound beef tenderloin steak, cut into ¼-inch-thick, ½-inch wide, and 2-inch-long strips
1 medium red bell pepper, stemmed, quartered, seeded, and cut crosswise into ¼-inch-wide strips
1 medium yellow bell pepper, stemmed, quartered, seeded, and cut crosswise into ¼-inch-wide strips
1 small red onion, thinly sliced
1 or 2 jalapeño chilies (according to taste), stemmed, seeded, and coarsely chopped
2 medium garlic cloves, finely chopped
1 teaspoon crushed red pepper flakes

1 teaspoon dried oregano
¼ cup olive oil
¼ cup lemon juice
4 (6-ounce) balls pizza dough; use a Standard or Sourdough Pizza crust (recipes on pages 14 and 16)
1 cup Tomato Sauce (recipe on page 18)
¼ cup plus 2 tablespoons chopped fresh cilantro leaves
¾ pound fresh mozzarella cheese, thinly sliced
2 medium-sized ripe avocados (preferably Haas)
¼ cup sour cream
2 medium scallions, finely chopped
Salt and freshly ground black pepper

Place a pizza brick, baking tiles, or a baking sheet in the oven and preheat the oven to 550°F.

In a mixing bowl, stir together the steak, red and yellow peppers, onion, chili, garlic, red pepper flakes, oregano, olive oil, and half the lemon juice. Marinate at room temperature for 15 to 30 minutes, turning two or three times.

Preheat the broiler until very hot, with the cooking surface close to the heat. Spread the steak fajita mixture evenly over the cooking surface and cook for about 2 minutes, turning the mixture once with a metal spatula. Remove from the heat.

Place a ball of dough on a work surface sprinkled with semolina. Using the heels of your hands, press down to flatten the dough. Lift and gently pull the dough to stretch it into a circle 8 inches in diameter. With your fingertips, press and shape a ½-inch rim around the crust. Repeat with remaining balls of dough.

Spread ¼ cup of the sauce on each piece of dough up to the rim. Scatter ¼ cup of the cilantro over the sauce, dividing it evenly among the pizzas. Place about a quarter of the mozzarella slices on top. Distribute the fajita mixture over the pizzas and top with the remaining cheese.

Carefully slide a pizza paddle under the pizzas, one at a time, and transfer them to the oven; with a slight push, slide each pizza off the paddle onto the baking surface. Bake the pizzas for 8 to 10 minutes or until the dough is browned and crisp and the cheese is golden and bubbly.

While the pizzas are baking, peel and seed the avocado and mash with the remaining lemon juice and cilantro, sour cream, scallion, and salt and pepper to taste. Before serving the pizzas, spread this guacamole mixture on top of each one.

Serves 4

GROUND BEEF, BLACK OLIVES, EGG, AND ONION

California-style in its far-ranging combination of ingredients, this pizza has a wonderfully homey, old-world quality.

May also be made as a calzone (see page 23).

¼ cup olive oil
4 medium garlic cloves, finely chopped
1 pound lean ground beef
2 (16-ounce) cans whole tomatoes
4 teaspoons double-concentrate tomato paste
4 teaspoons sugar
4 teaspoons dried oregano
1 teaspoon crushed red pepper flakes
½ teaspoon salt

4 (6-ounce) balls pizza dough; use a Standard, Whole-Wheat, or Sourdough Pizza Crust (recipes on pages 14–16)
48 Niçoise olives or other marinated black olives, halved and pitted
4 hard-boiled eggs, shelled and cut into ¼-inch-thick slices
1½ cups thinly sliced red onion
¾ pound mozzarella cheese, shredded

In a large saucepan, heat the oil over medium heat. Add the garlic and sauté about 1 minute. Raise the heat slightly, add the beef, and sauté until lightly browned, about 5 minutes, stirring frequently with a wooden spoon to break up the beef into small, thumbnail-sized clumps. Carefully pour off the excess fat from the pan.

Add the tomatoes, breaking them up with your fingers. Stir in the tomato paste, oregano, red pepper flakes, and salt. Simmer briskly, stirring frequently, until the mixture has reduced to a thick sauce with no excess liquid, 15 to 20 minutes. Remove the pan from the heat.

Place a pizza brick, baking tiles, or a baking sheet in the oven and preheat the oven to 550°F.

Place a ball of dough on a work surface sprinkled with semolina. Using the heels of your hands, press down to flatten the dough. Lift and gently pull the dough to stretch it into a circle 8 inches in diameter. With your fingertips, press and shape a ½-inch rim around the crust. Repeat with remaining balls of dough.

Spread one quarter of the meat mixture on each piece of dough up to the rim.

Distribute the pitted olives on top of each pizza, pushing them down into the sauce. Arrange the egg slices on top of each, then the onions. Top each pizza with the mozzarella.

Carefully slide a pizza paddle under the pizzas, one at a time, and transfer them to the oven; with a slight push, slide each pizza off the paddle onto the baking surface. Bake the pizzas for 8 to 10 minutes or until the dough is browned and crisp and the cheese is golden and bubbly.

Serves 4

SMOKED BEEF, SUN-DRIED TOMATOES, AND PECORINO WITH PEPPER

A well-stocked deli will have some form of cured smoked beef. If it's unavailable, substitute smoked pork and have it sliced paper-thin.

The intensity of the sun-dried tomatoes, the sharp tang of the pecorino—an aged sheep's milk cheese often mixed with cracked black peppercorns—and the wonderfully aromatic Pesto Sauce complement the beef perfectly and give this pizza a deliciously distinctive flavor.

4 (6-ounce) balls pizza dough; use a Sourdough or Standard Pizza Crust (recipes on pages 16 and 14)
1 cup Pesto Sauce (recipe on page 20)
¼ pound pecorino cheese with black peppercorns, grated
Freshly ground black pepper (optional)
32 sun-dried tomato pieces
¼ pound cured smoked beef, thinly sliced
¾ pound mozzarella cheese, shredded

Place a pizza brick, baking tiles, or a baking sheet in the oven and preheat the oven to 550°F.

Place a ball of dough on a work surface sprinkled with semolina. Using the heels of your hands, press down to flatten the dough. Lift and gently pull the dough to stretch it into a circle 8 inches in diameter. With your fingertips, press and shape a ½-inch rim around the crust. Repeat with remaining balls of dough. Spread ¼ cup of the sauce on each piece of dough up to the rim.

Sprinkle the grated pecorino cheese equally on each pizza. (If the pecorino cheese does not have black peppercorns in it, coarsely grind black pepper over the cheese.)

Arrange the sun-dried tomato pieces on top of the cheese. Then cover these toppings with the sliced beef, overlapping the slices slightly. Top each pizza with shredded mozzarella.

Carefully slide a pizza paddle under the pizzas, one at a time, and transfer them to the oven; with a slight push, slide each pizza off the paddle onto the baking surface. Bake the pizzas for 8 to 10 minutes or until the dough is browned and crisp and the cheese is golden and bubbly.

Serves 4

CANADIAN BACON, EGG, AND CHEDDAR

Who says you can't eat pizza for breakfast? This beats the breakfast sandwiches you get at most fast-food places, though you do have to eat it with a knife and fork.

4 (6-ounce) balls pizza dough; use a Sourdough, Whole-Wheat, or Standard Pizza crust (recipes on pages 14–16)

1 cup Tomato Sauce (recipe on page 18)

½ cup grated Parmesan cheese

¼ cup unsalted butter

4 large eggs

¾ pound well-trimmed Canadian bacon, cut into ¼-inch-thick slices

½ pound sharp cheddar cheese, thinly sliced

Place a pizza brick, baking tiles, or a baking sheet in the oven and preheat the oven to 550°F.

Place a ball of dough on a work surface sprinkled with semolina. Using the heels of your hands, press down to flatten the dough. Lift and gently pull the dough to stretch it into a circle 8 inches in diameter. With your fingertips, press and shape a ½-inch rim around the crust. Repeat with remaining balls of dough. Spread ¼ cup of the sauce on each piece of dough up to the rim. Sprinkle the Parmesan over the sauce on each.

In a frying pan, preferably nonstick, melt 1 tablespoon of the butter over medium-to-low heat. Carefully break 1 egg into the pan and fry it, tilting and swirling it so the white spreads out. Using a small spoon, baste the egg with butter from the pan. As soon as the white has set, about 1 minute, use a spatula to carefully transfer the egg to the top of one pizza; don't worry if the yolk breaks. Repeat until each pizza is capped with an egg.

Distribute the Canadian bacon slices evenly over each pizza, covering the eggs and any sauce that shows around them. Cover the bacon with the cheddar slices.

Carefully slide a pizza paddle under the pizzas, one at a time, and transfer them to the oven; with a slight push, slide each pizza off the paddle onto the baking surface. Bake the pizzas for 8 to 10 minutes or until the dough is browned and crisp and the cheese is golden and bubbly.

Serves 4

PROSCIUTTO AND FONTINA WITH MARINATED OLIVES

The intense flavors of thinly sliced Italian prosciutto and briny olives are thrown into sharp relief by mild fontina cheese on this sauceless pizza.

4 (6-ounce) balls pizza dough; use a Sourdough or Standard Pizza Crust (recipes on pages 16 and 14)

¾ pound fontina cheese, shredded

6 ounces prosciutto, thinly sliced

½ pound mozzarella cheese, shredded

32 marinated Italian olives, halved and pitted

4 teaspoons dried oregano

Place a pizza brick, baking tiles, or a baking sheet in the oven and preheat the oven to 550°F.

Place a ball of dough on a work surface sprinkled with semolina. Using the heels of your hands, press down to flatten the dough. Lift and gently pull the dough to stretch it into a circle 8 inches in diameter. With your fingertips, press and shape a ½-inch rim around the crust. Repeat with remaining balls of dough. Spread one quarter of the fontina on each piece of dough up to the rim.

Top the cheese on each pizza with the sliced prosciutto. Then cover the prosciutto with the mozzarella, dot with the olive halves, and crumble the oregano on top.

Carefully slide a pizza paddle under the pizzas, one at a time, and transfer them to the oven; with a slight push, slide each pizza off the paddle onto the baking surface. Bake the pizzas for 8 to 10 minutes or until the dough is browned and crisp and the cheese is golden and bubbly.

Serves 4

CLASSIC PEPPERONI

Even the most modern of California pizza lovers occasionally succumbs to a classic topping like this.

4 (6-ounce) balls pizza dough; use a Sourdough, Whole-Wheat, or Standard Pizza Crust (recipes on pages 14–16)

1 cup Tomato Sauce (recipe on page 18)

½ cup grated Parmesan cheese

4 ounces pepperoni sausage, peeled and thinly sliced (about 10 slices to the inch)

6 ounces provolone cheese, shredded

6 ounces mozzarella cheese, shredded

Place a pizza brick, baking tiles, or a baking sheet in the oven and preheat the oven to 550°F.

Place a ball of dough on a work surface sprinkled with semolina. Using the heels of your hands, press down to flatten the dough. Lift and gently pull the dough to stretch it into a circle 8 inches in diameter. With your fingertips, press and shape a ½-inch rim around the crust. Repeat with remaining balls of dough. Spread ¼ cup of the sauce on each piece of dough up to the rim.

Sprinkle the Parmesan over the sauce on each pizza and distribute the pepperoni slices on top. Cover each pizza with the grated provolone and mozzarella.

Carefully slide a pizza paddle under the pizzas, one at a time, and transfer them to the oven; with a slight push, slide each pizza off the paddle onto the baking surface. Bake the pizzas for 8 to 10 minutes or until the dough is browned and crisp and the cheese is golden and bubbly.

Serves 4

HOT ITALIAN SAUSAGE,
SWEET RED PEPPERS, AND MAUI ONIONS

If you can't get Maui onions, use Vidalia, Walla Walla, or the sweetest brown-skinned onions you can find.

4 fresh hot Italian sausages, 3½ to 4 ounces each
4 (6-ounce) balls pizza dough; use a Sourdough or Standard Pizza Crust (recipes on pages 16 and 14)
1 cup Tomato Sauce (recipe on page 18)

½ pound mozzarella cheese, shredded
4 medium red bell peppers, roasted (recipe on page 22) and torn into ¼-inch-wide strips
2 medium Maui onions, thinly sliced
¼ pound Romano cheese, shaved or shredded

Place a pizza brick, baking tiles, or a baking sheet in the oven and preheat the oven to 550°F.

Preheat the grill or broiler until very hot, with the cooking surface close to the heat.

Put the sausages in a saucepan and add enough cold water to cover them. Cover the pan and bring the water to a boil over moderate heat. As soon as the water boils, drain the sausages. With a fork, puncture each sausage in a few places and transfer to the grill or broiler. Cook the sausages for 1½ to 2 minutes per side, until their skins are just browned.

Place a ball of dough on a work surface sprinkled with semolina. Using the heels of your hands, press down to flatten the dough. Lift and gently pull the dough to stretch it into a circle 8 inches in diameter. With your fingertips, press and shape a ½-inch rim around the crust. Repeat with remaining balls of dough.

Spread ¼ cup of the sauce on each piece of dough up to the rim. Using half of the mozzarella, sprinkle an equal portion on each pizza.

With a sharp knife held at a 45-degree angle, cut the sausages into ¼- to ½-inch-thick slices. Distribute them on the pizzas. Scatter the roasted pepper strips and onions on top. Then sprinkle each with the remaining mozzarella and Romano.

Carefully slide a pizza paddle under the pizzas, one at a time, and transfer them to the oven; with a slight push, slide each pizza off the paddle onto the baking surface. Bake the pizzas for 8 to 10 minutes or until the dough is browned and crisp and the cheese is golden and bubbly.

Serves 4

ANDOUILLE SAUSAGE WITH VIDALIA ONIONS, CORN, AND GREEN PEPPER

The popularity of Cajun cuisine has brought spicy andouille sausage to most good butcher shops and gourmet markets. If you can't find it, substitute hot Italian sausage.

The sweetness of corn and good southern Vidalia onions (substitute Maui or Walla Walla onions or the sweetest you can find) and the piquancy of green bell pepper make for a tasty combination.

4 fresh andouille sausages, about 4 ounces each

4 (6-ounce) balls pizza dough; use Standard or Sourdough Pizza Crusts (recipes on pages 14 and 16)

1 cup Tomato Sauce (recipe on page 18)

¾ teaspoon ground red pepper

½ teaspoon freshly ground white pepper

½ teaspoon ground dried cumin

1 (8¾-ounce) can sweet corn, drained

1 medium green bell pepper, stemmed, quartered, seeded, and cut crosswise into ¼-inch-wide strips

1½ cups thinly sliced Vidalia onion

¾ pound mozzarella cheese, shredded

Place a pizza brick, baking tiles, or a baking sheet in the oven and preheat the oven to 550°F.

Preheat the grill or broiler until very hot, with the cooking surface close to the heat.

Put the sausages in a saucepan and add enough cold water to cover them. Cover the pan and bring the water to a boil over moderate heat. As soon as the water boils, drain the sausages. With a fork, puncture each sausage in a few places and transfer to the grill or broiler. Cook the sausages for 1½ to 2 minutes per side, until their skins are just browned.

Place a ball of dough on a work surface sprinkled with semolina. Using the heels of your hands, press down to flatten the dough. Lift and gently pull the dough to stretch it into a circle 8 inches in diameter. With your fingertips, press and shape a ½-inch rim around the crust. Repeat with remaining balls of dough.

Spread ¼ cup of the sauce on each piece of dough up to the rim. Evenly sprinkle the red and white pepper and the cumin over the sauce on each crust. Scatter the corn on top of each pizza, then the bell pepper and onion.

With a sharp knife held at a 45-degree angle, cut the sausages into ¼-inch-thick slices. Distribute the slices on each pizza. Scatter the mozzarella on top.

Carefully slide a pizza paddle under the pizzas, one at a time, and transfer them to the oven; with a slight push, slide each pizza off the paddle onto the baking surface. Bake the pizzas for 8 to 10 minutes or until the dough is browned and crisp and the cheese is golden and bubbly.

Serves 4

VEAL MEATBALL WITH ENOKI MUSHROOMS, HERBS, AND RICOTTA

The combination of light veal meatballs and enoki mushrooms with a creamy Tomato Sauce gives this pizza a nouvelle flair.

May also be made as a calzone (see page 23).

1 pound ground veal
½ cup fine cracker crumbs (use saltines or water biscuits)
1 large egg, beaten until frothy
6 tablespoons heavy cream
¼ teaspoon dried oregano
¼ teaspoon dried rosemary
¼ teaspoon dried thyme
¼ teaspoon dried savory
¼ teaspoon salt

¼ teaspoon freshly ground white pepper
¼ cup olive oil
4 (6-ounce) balls pizza dough; use a Standard Pizza Crust (recipe on page 14)
¾ cup crème fraîche or heavy cream
¾ pound enoki mushrooms
¾ pound ricotta cheese
6 ounces mozzarella cheese, shredded

Place a pizza brick, baking tiles, or a baking sheet in the oven and preheat the oven to 550°F.

Preheat the broiler until very hot, with the cooking surface close to the heat.

In a mixing bowl, combine the veal, cracker crumbs, egg, cream, herbs, salt, and pepper, mixing with your hands until smooth.

Pour the oil onto a dinner plate. Lightly moisten your fingertips with the oil and shape the veal mixture into balls about 1 inch in diameter. Then roll the balls in the oil to coat them evenly.

Place the meatballs under the broiler until they are golden, about 2 minutes per side. Remove and set them aside.

Place a ball of dough on a work surface sprinkled with semolina. Using the heels of your hands, press down to flatten the dough. Lift and gently pull the dough to stretch it into a circle 8 inches in diameter. With your fingertips, press and shape a ½-inch rim around the crust. Repeat with remaining balls of dough. Stir together the Tomato Sauce and crème fraîche; spread one quarter of this mixture on each piece of dough up to the rim.

Divide the meatballs evenly among the pizzas. Gently press them down as you put them on the pizzas to flatten them slightly. Distribute small clusters of enoki mushrooms in between the meatballs. Dot the ricotta evenly over the pizzas, then top each with one quarter of the mozzarella.

Carefully slide a pizza paddle under the pizzas, one at a time, and transfer them to the oven; with a slight push, slide each pizza off the paddle onto the baking surface. Bake the pizzas for 8 to 10 minutes or until the dough is browned and crisp and the cheese is golden and bubbly.

Serves 4

On preceding page:
Grilled Shrimp with Sun-Dried Tomatoes, Pesto, and Ricotta (page 66)
At left:
Smoked Salmon, Boursin, Chives, and Salmon Caviar (page 85)

WHITE VEAL SAUSAGE WITH MUSTARD, YELLOW BELL PEPPERS, AND BRIE

These pizzas with a Middle-European flair have slices of grilled bratwurst and a subtle sauce of mustard mixed with French crème fraîche. They are topped with mild, creamy Brie cheese. If you can't find the crème fraîche—a product similar to slightly soured heavy cream—substitute equal parts of lightly whipped heavy cream and sour cream.

Buy a little more than ¾ pound of a good, ripe Brie—the weight given is for the cheese trimmed of its white rind. You can substitute fontina for the Brie.

With the creamy sauce, the toppings may slip off the crust if you try to lift a piece so use a knife and fork to eat this pizza.

4 fresh bratwurst (white veal sausages), 3½ to 4 ounces each	½ cup freshly grated Parmesan cheese
4 (6-ounce) balls pizza dough; use a Standard Crust (recipe on page 14)	2 medium yellow bell peppers, stemmed, quartered, seeded, and cut crosswise into ¼-inch-wide strips
1 cup crème fraîche	
¼ cup grainy Dijon-style mustard	¾ pound trimmed ripe Brie cheese

Place a pizza brick, baking tiles, or a baking sheet in the oven and preheat the oven to 550°F.

Preheat the grill or broiler until very hot, with the cooking surface close to the heat.

Put the sausages in a saucepan and add enough cold water to cover them. Cover the pan and bring the water to a boil over moderate heat. As soon as the water boils, drain the sausages. With a fork, puncture each sausage in a few places and transfer them to the grill or broiler. Cook them for 1½ to 2 minutes per side, until their skins are just browned.

Place a ball of dough on a work surface sprinkled with semolina. Using the heels of your hands, press down to flatten the dough. Lift and gently pull the dough to stretch it into a circle 8 inches in diameter. With your fingertips, press and shape a ½-inch rim around the crust. Repeat with remaining balls of dough.

Stir together the crème fraîche and mustard; spread one quarter of the mixture on each piece of dough up to the rim. Sprinkle the Parmesan on top.

Cut the sausages with a sharp knife held at a 45-degree angle into ¼ to ½-inch-thick slices. Distribute the slices on each pizza. Scatter the yellow pepper strips on top and dot each pizza evenly with the Brie, pinching off pieces of the cheese with your fingers.

Carefully slide a pizza paddle under the pizzas, one at a time, and transfer them to the oven; with a slight push, slide each pizza off the paddle onto the baking surface. Bake the pizzas for 8 to 10 minutes or until the dough is browned and crisp and the cheese is golden and bubbly.

Serves 4

MARINATED LAMB WITH BLACK OLIVES, ROASTED PEPPERS, AND FETA

Typical Greek ingredients and seasonings—lamb, feta, olives, and oregano—give this pizza an Eastern Mediterranean flavor. If you can't get a whole piece of lamb tenderloin, you can use good lamb chops. In that case, be sure you get enough to yield the right amount of meat after bone and fat have been trimmed. A typical 3½-ounce chop gives you about 2½ ounces of trimmed meat.

¼ cup olive oil
2 tablespoons lemon juice
4 teaspoons dried oregano
¾ pound tenderloin of lamb, trimmed
Salt and freshly ground black pepper
4 (6-ounce) balls pizza dough; use a Standard or Sourdough Pizza Crust (recipes on pages 14 and 16)

1 cup Tomato Sauce (recipe on page 18)
10 ounces mozzarella cheese, shredded
4 medium red bell peppers, roasted (recipe on page 22) and torn into ½-inch-wide strips
12 ounces feta cheese
48 Greek olives, halved and pitted

Place a pizza brick, baking tiles, or a baking sheet in the oven and preheat the oven to 550°F.

In a bowl, stir together the olive oil and lemon juice; crumble in 2 teaspoons of the oregano. Add the lamb and turn to coat evenly. Marinate at room temperature for 15 to 30 minutes, turning the lamb two or three times.

Preheat the grill or broiler until very hot, with the cooking surface close to the heat. Sprinkle the lamb with salt and pepper and grill or broil the lamb 1 to 1½ minutes per side, until it is seared but still pink. With a sharp knife held at a 45-degree angle, carve the lamb crosswise into ¼-inch-thick slices.

Place a ball of dough on a work surface sprinkled with semolina. Using the heels of your hands, press down to flatten the dough. Lift and gently pull the dough to stretch it into a circle 8 inches in diameter. With your fingertips, press and shape a ½-inch rim around the crust. Repeat with remaining balls of dough.

Spread ¼ cup of the sauce on each piece of dough up to the rim. Distribute 1 ounce of the mozzarella on each pizza. Then arrange the lamb slices on top of each, followed by the pepper strips.

Crumble the feta over the lamb on each pizza. Sprinkle the pizzas with the remaining oregano, top with the remaining mozzarella, and dot with olive halves.

Carefully slide a pizza paddle under the pizzas, one at a time, and transfer them to the oven; with a slight push, slide each pizza off the paddle onto the baking surface. Bake the pizzas for 8 to 10 minutes or until the dough is browned and crisp and the cheese is golden and bubbly.

Serves 4

GROUND LAMB WITH EGGPLANT, PESTO, AND PINE NUTS

Some tasters claim this pizza has a Middle Eastern flavor. Others say it reminds them of Indian cuisine. In truth, it shows influences of both regions.
May also be made as a calzone (see page 23).

¼ cup olive oil
4 medium garlic cloves, finely chopped
1 teaspoon ground cumin
1 teaspoon ground chili powder
½ teaspoon ground coriander
1 pound lean ground lamb
1 teaspoon dried oregano
½ teaspoon salt
½ teaspoon freshly ground black pepper

¾ pound Japanese eggplant, peeled and cut lengthwise into ¼-inch-thick slices
¼ cup sesame oil
4 (6-ounce) balls pizza dough; use a Standard, Sourdough, or Whole-Wheat Pizza Crust (recipes on pages 14–16)
1 cup Pesto Sauce (recipe on page 20)
¾ pound mozzarella cheese, shredded
⅓ cup pine nuts

In a large saucepan, heat the oil over medium heat. Add the garlic and sauté about 1 minute. Add the cumin, chili powder, and coriander; sauté about 30 seconds more. Add the lamb, oregano, salt, and pepper, sauté until browned, 5 to 7 minutes, stirring frequently with a wooden spoon to break up the lamb thoroughly. Carefully pour off the excess fat from the pan.

Place a pizza brick, baking tiles, or a baking sheet in the oven and preheat the oven to 550°F. Preheat the grill or broiler until very hot, with the cooking surface close to the heat.

Brush the eggplant slices with the sesame oil and grill or broil them until golden, about 1 minute per side.

Place a ball of dough on a work surface sprinkled with semolina. Using the heels of your hands, press down to flatten the dough. Lift and gently pull the dough to stretch it into a circle 8 inches in diameter. With your fingertips, press and shape a ½-inch rim around the crust. Repeat with remaining balls of dough.

Spread ¼ cup of the sauce on each piece of dough up to the rim. Sprinkle the lamb mixture over the pizzas, gently pressing the meat into the sauce. Using about one quarter of the cheese, sprinkle an equal portion of it on each pizza. Place the eggplant slices on top, then scatter the rest of the cheese and the pine nuts over the pizzas.

Carefully slide a pizza paddle under the pizzas, one at a time, and transfer them to the oven; with a slight push, slide each pizza off the paddle onto the baking surface. Bake the pizzas for 8 to 10 minutes or until the dough is browned and crisp and the cheese is golden and bubbly.

Serves 4

5
SEAFOOD TOPPINGS

GRILLED SHRIMP WITH RED BELL PEPPER PUREE AND SWEET ONIONS
GRILLED SHRIMP WITH SUN-DRIED TOMATOES, PESTO, AND RICOTTA
CAJUN SHRIMP
SESAME SHRIMP TERIYAKI
GRILLED SCALLOPS WITH PESTO, SUN-DRIED TOMATOES, AND FONTINA
GRILLED SCALLOPS WITH RED AND YELLOW PEPPERS
LOBSTER WITH SUN-DRIED TOMATOES, BASIL, AND FRESH MOZZARELLA
LOBSTER WITH FRESH TOMATOES, ROASTED GARLIC, AND FONTINA
CRAB, PINE NUTS, ROASTED CHILIES, AND GOAT CHEESE
CRAB WITH LEMON BUTTER AND FRESH MOZZARELLA
CAVIAR AND CREME FRAICHE

CLAM AND GARLIC-HERB BUTTER
RED CLAM WITH FRESH GARLIC AND RED PEPPER
SMOKED OYSTERS WITH PROVOLONE AND SMOKED MOZZARELLA
SMOKED SALMON, BOURSIN, CHIVES, AND SALMON CAVIAR
SMOKED SALMON WITH CREME FRAICHE, LEMON ZEST, AND CAPERS
TUNA AND PROVOLONE
ANCHOVIES AND GOLDEN ONIONS
ANCHOVIES, HERBS, AND RICOTTA
ANCHOVIES WITH BLACK OLIVE PESTO
ANCHOVIES, ROASTED GARLIC, AND THREE CHEESES

GRILLED SHRIMP WITH
RED BELL PEPPER PUREE AND SWEET ONIONS

A visual surprise here: although the sauce looks like tomato, it's actually a puree of roasted red bell peppers with the sharp tang of lemon juice and cilantro. It's a great background for butterflied shrimp and sweet onions—whether Mauis, Vidalias, Walla Wallas, or the sweetest brown-skinned onions you can find.

32 medium-to-large fresh shrimp (about ¾ pound), peeled and cleaned
6 tablespoons olive oil
¼ cup lemon juice
Salt and freshly ground black pepper
4 medium red bell peppers, roasted (recipe on page 22)
1½ tablespoons fresh cilantro leaves

4 (6-ounce) balls pizza dough; use a Standard or Sourdough Pizza Crust (recipes on pages 14 and 16)
¾ pound mozzarella cheese, shredded
1 medium Maui onion, thinly sliced

Place a pizza brick, baking tiles, or a baking sheet in the oven and preheat the oven to 550°F.

Slit each shrimp halfway through along its outer curve and open it out to "butterfly" it. Put the shrimp in a nonreactive bowl. Toss the shrimp with half the olive oil and half the lemon juice to coat the shrimp well. Marinate at room temperature for about 15 minutes, turning the shrimp two or three times.

Preheat the grill or broiler until very hot, with the cooking surface close to the heat. In four batches, sprinkle the shrimp with salt and pepper to taste and grill or broil them for about 30 seconds per side, initially placing them slit sides down on the cooking surface.

To make the sauce, put the roasted peppers, cilantro, and remaining oil and lemon juice in a food processor fitted with the metal blade. Add salt and pepper to taste and process continuously until smooth.

Place a ball of dough on a work surface sprinkled with semolina. Using the heels of your hands, press down to flatten the dough. Lift and gently pull the dough to stretch it into a circle 8 inches in diameter. With your fingertips, press and shape a ½-inch rim around the crust. Repeat with remaining balls of dough. Spread one quarter of the sauce on each piece of dough up to the rim.

Using a third of the mozzarella, spread an equal amount of it on each pizza. Top each with onion. Place the shrimp on the pizzas and top with the remaining mozzarella.

Carefully slide a pizza paddle under the pizzas, one at a time, and transfer them to the oven; with a slight push, slide each pizza off the paddle onto the baking surface. Bake the pizzas for 8 to 10 minutes or until the dough is browned and crisp and the cheese is golden and bubbly.

Serves 4

GRILLED SHRIMP WITH SUN-DRIED TOMATOES, PESTO, AND RICOTTA

Shrimp and sun-dried tomatoes are a great pairing. The Pesto Sauce and ricotta provide the perfect background.
May also be made as a calzone (see page 23).

32 medium-to-large fresh shrimp (about ¾ pound) peeled, cleaned, and each shrimp cut into two or three pieces
3 tablespoons olive oil
2 tablespoons lemon juice
Salt and freshly ground black pepper
4 (6-ounce) balls pizza dough; use a Standard or

Sourdough Pizza Crust (recipes on pages 14 and 16)
1 cup Pesto Sauce (recipe on page 20)
¼ pound provolone cheese, shredded
32 sun-dried tomato pieces
10 ounces part-skim-milk ricotta cheese
6 ounces mozzarella cheese, shredded

Place a pizza brick, baking tiles, or a baking sheet in the oven and preheat the oven to 550°F.

Put the shrimp in a nonreactive bowl. Toss the shrimp with the olive oil and lemon juice to coat them well. Marinate at room temperature for about 15 minutes, turning the shrimp two or three times.

Preheat the grill or broiler until very hot, with the cooking surface close to the heat. In four batches, sprinkle the shrimp with salt and pepper to taste and grill or broil them for about one minute, turning them once.

Place a ball of dough on a work surface sprinkled with semolina. Using the heels of your hands, press down to flatten the dough. Lift and gently pull the dough to stretch it into a circle 8 inches in diameter. With your fingertips, press and shape a ½-inch rim around the crust. Repeat with remaining balls of dough. Spread ¼ cup of the sauce on each piece of dough up to the rim.

Sprinkle the provolone on each pizza. Scatter the shrimp pieces and the sun-dried tomatoes on top of each and then dot with the ricotta. Sprinkle the mozzarella evenly over each pizza.

Carefully slide a pizza paddle under the pizzas, one at a time, and transfer them to the oven; with a slight push, slide each pizza off the paddle onto the baking surface. Bake the pizzas for 8 to 10 minutes or until the dough is browned and crisp and the cheese is golden and bubbly.

Serves 4

CAJUN SHRIMP

Spicy shrimp are a standard in the Cajun kitchen and, thus, a logical topping for a California-style pizza!

32 medium-to-large fresh shrimp (about ¾ pound), peeled and cleaned
¼ cup vegetable oil
½ tablespoon ground red pepper
1 teaspoon freshly ground white pepper
1 teaspoon ground cumin
½ teaspoon salt

4 (6-ounce) balls pizza dough; use a Standard or Sourdough Pizza Crust (recipes on pages 14 and 16)
1 cup Tomato Sauce (recipe on page 18)
¾ pound mozzarella cheese, shredded
2 medium red bell peppers, roasted (recipe on page 22) and torn into ½-inch-wide strips

Place a pizza brick, baking tiles, or a baking sheet in the oven and preheat the oven to 550°F.

Slit each shrimp halfway through along its outer curve and open it out to "butterfly" it. Put the shrimp in a bowl. Toss the shrimp with the oil, half the red and white peppers, and half the cumin to coat the shrimp well. Marinate at room temperature for about 15 minutes, turning the shrimp two or three times.

Preheat the grill or broiler until very hot, with the cooking surface close to the heat. In four batches, sprinkle the shrimp with salt to taste and grill or broil them for about 30 seconds per side, initially placing them slit sides down on the cooking surface.

Place a ball of dough on a work surface sprinkled with semolina. Using the heels of your hands, press down to flatten the dough. Lift and gently pull the dough to stretch it into a circle 8 inches in diameter. With your fingertips, press and shape a ½-inch rim around the crust. Repeat with remaining balls of dough.

Spread ¼ cup of the sauce on each piece of dough up to the rim. Sprinkle each pizza evenly with the remaining spices. Using about one-third of the mozzarella, sprinkle an equal portion of it on each pizza.

Place the shrimp on each pizza. Scatter the roasted pepper strips evenly over the pizzas, then top with the remaining cheese.

Carefully slide a pizza paddle under the pizzas, one at a time, and transfer them to the oven; with a slight push, slide each pizza off the paddle onto the baking surface. Bake the pizzas for 8 to 10 minutes or until the dough is browned and crisp and the cheese is golden and bubbly.

Serves 4

SESAME SHRIMP TERIYAKI

The sweet-salty flavor of teriyaki and plum sauces go splendidly with fresh, plump shrimp. Use the best commercially prepared sauces you can find in the Asian food section of your supermarket.

32 medium-to-large fresh shrimp (about ¾ pound), peeled and cleaned
¼ cup teriyaki sauce
2 tablespoons sesame oil
4 (6-ounce) balls pizza dough; use a Standard or Sourdough Pizza Crust (recipes on pages 14 and 16)
1 cup plum sauce

4 medium scallions, finely chopped
¾ pound mozzarella cheese, shredded
2 medium yellow or red bell peppers, stemmed, quartered, seeded, and cut crosswise into ¼-inch-wide strips
¼ cup sesame seeds

Place a pizza brick, baking tiles, or a baking sheet in the oven and preheat the oven to 550°F.

Slit each shrimp halfway through along its outer curve and open it out to "butterfly" it. Put the shrimp in a bowl. Toss the shrimp with the teriyaki sauce and sesame oil to coat them well. Marinate at room temperature for about 15 minutes, turning the shrimp two or three times.

Preheat the grill or broiler until very hot, with the cooking surface close to the heat. In four batches, grill or broil the shrimp for about 30 seconds per side, initially placing them slit sides down on the cooking surface.

Place a ball of dough on a work surface sprinkled with semolina. Using the heels of your hands, press down to flatten the dough. Lift and gently pull the dough to stretch it into a circle 8 inches in diameter. With your fingertips, press and shape a ½-inch rim around the crust. Repeat with remaining balls of dough. Spread ¼ cup of the sauce up to the rim on each piece of dough.

Scatter the scallions on each pizza. Then using about a third of the cheese, sprinkle an equal amount of it on each pizza. Place the shrimp on top. Add the

pepper strips and top each pizza with the remaining cheese. Sprinkle the sesame seeds evenly over each pizza.

Carefully slide a pizza paddle under the pizzas, one at a time, and transfer them to the oven; with a slight push, slide each pizza off the paddle onto the baking surface. Bake the pizzas for 8 to 10 minutes or until the dough is browned and crisp and the cheese is golden and bubbly.

Serves 4

On preceding page:
Marinated Olives, Peppers, and Sun-Dried Tomatoes (page 98)
At left:
Hearts of Palm, Artichoke Hearts, Fontina, and Pesto (page 100)

LOBSTER WITH SUN-DRIED TOMATOES, BASIL, AND FRESH MOZZARELLA

The rich, distinctive flavor of fresh lobster tail gets a Mediterranean treatment here by contrasting it with the vibrant tastes of sun-dried tomatoes and fresh basil and the purity of fresh buffalo mozzarella.

A good fish market will have fresh or frozen lobster tails for sale. My local one usually stocks Australian rock lobster tails, which are a good alternative to standard American lobster.

¾–1 pound of lobster tails in the shell (to yield roughly 10–14 ounces shelled, uncooked meat)

3 tablespoons olive oil

1 tablespoon lemon juice

Salt and freshly ground black pepper

4 (6-ounce) balls pizza dough; use a Standard Pizza Crust (recipe on page 14)

1 cup Tomato Sauce (recipe on page 18)

32 sun-dried tomato pieces

16 fresh basil leaves, rolled and cut crosswise into julienne strips

1 pound fresh buffalo mozzarella, cut into ¼-inch-thick slices

Place a pizza brick, baking tiles, or a baking sheet in the oven and preheat the oven to 550°F.

With the tip of a small, sharp knife, carefully cut through the shells lengthwise along the underside of each lobster tail. With your thumbs, carefully pry apart the shells and peel them away from the meat.

Slice the meat crosswise into ½-inch-thick medallions; don't worry if some of the medallions fall apart into smaller pieces. Put the lobster pieces in a nonreactive bowl. Toss the lobster with the olive oil and lemon juice to coat it well. Marinate at room temperature for about 15 minutes, turning the lobster pieces two or three times.

Preheat the grill or broiler until very hot, with the cooking surface close to the heat. In four batches, sprinkle the lobster with salt and pepper to taste and grill or broil for about 30 seconds per side, until just seared.

Place a ball of dough on a work surface sprinkled with semolina. Using the heels of your hands, press down to flatten the dough. Lift and gently pull the

dough to stretch it into a circle 8 inches in diameter. With your fingertips, press and shape a ½-inch rim around the crust. Repeat with remaining balls of dough.

Spread ¼ cup of the sauce on each piece of dough up to the rim. Place the sun-dried tomatoes on top of each and scatter the basil over the pizzas.

Distribute the pieces of lobster evenly among the pizzas. Place the sliced mozzarella on top, covering the lobster.

Carefully slide a pizza paddle under the pizzas, one at a time, and transfer them to the oven; with a slight push, slide each pizza off the paddle onto the baking surface. Bake the pizzas for 8 to 10 minutes or until the dough is browned and crisp and the cheese is golden and bubbly.

Serves 4

LOBSTER WITH FRESH TOMATOES, ROASTED GARLIC, AND FONTINA

The refined flavor of Roasted Garlic Cloves is a lovely complement to the sweet, rich flavor of lobster tails.

¾–1 pound of lobster tails in the shell (to yield roughly 10–14 ounces shelled, uncooked meat)

3 tablespoons olive oil from Roasted Garlic Cloves (recipe on page 21)

1 tablespoon lemon juice

Salt and freshly ground black pepper

4 (6-ounce) balls pizza dough; use a Standard Pizza Crust (recipe on page 14)

32 medium Roasted Garlic Cloves (recipe on page 21)

6 ounces fontina cheese, shredded

½ pound firm, ripe Roma tomatoes, cored and cut crosswise into ¼-inch-thick slices

2 teaspoons chopped fresh oregano leaves (or 1 teaspoon dried)

6 ounces mozzarella cheese, shredded

Place a pizza brick, baking tiles, or a baking sheet in the oven and preheat the oven to 550°F.

With the tip of a small, sharp knife, carefully cut through the shells lengthwise along the underside of each lobster tail. With your thumbs, carefully pry apart the shells and peel them away from the meat.

Slice the meat crosswise into ½-inch-thick medallions; don't worry if some of the medallions fall apart into smaller pieces. Put the lobster pieces in a nonreactive bowl. Toss the lobster with the olive oil and lemon juice to coat it well. Marinate at room temperature for about 15 minutes, turning the lobster pieces two or three times.

Preheat the grill or broiler until very hot, with the cooking surface close to the heat. In four batches, sprinkle the lobster with salt and pepper to taste and grill or broil for about 30 seconds per side, until just seared.

Place a ball of dough on a work surface sprinkled with semolina. Using the heels of your hands, press down to flatten the dough. Lift and gently pull the dough to stretch it into a circle 8 inches in diameter. With your fingertips, press and shape a ½-inch rim around the crust. Repeat with remaining balls of dough.

Distribute the Roasted Garlic Cloves over the pizzas, pressing down gently to spread them out. Sprinkle on the fontina; then place the tomato slices on top and sprinkle each pizza with oregano.

Distribute the pieces of lobster evenly among the pizzas. Spread the mozzarella on top.

Carefully slide a pizza paddle under the pizzas, one at a time, and transfer them to the oven; with a slight push, slide each pizza off the paddle onto the baking surface. Bake the pizzas for 8 to 10 minutes or until the dough is browned and crisp and the cheese is golden and bubbly.

Serves 4

GRILLED SCALLOPS WITH RED AND YELLOW PEPPERS

Scallops and peppers share a wonderful sweetness. Buy fresh sea scallops at least 1 inch in diameter; you can also use fresh-frozen scallops.

1 pound large sea scallops
3 tablespoons olive oil
1 tablespoon lemon juice
¼ teaspoon dried oregano
¼ teaspoon dried thyme
¼ teaspoon dried rosemary
¼ teaspoon dried savory
Salt and freshly ground black pepper
4 (6-ounce) balls pizza dough; use a Standard or Sourdough Pizza Crust (recipes on pages 14 and 16)

1 cup Tomato Sauce (recipe on page 18)
¾ pound mozzarella cheese, shredded
1 red bell pepper, stemmed, quartered, seeded, and cut crosswise into ¼-inch-wide strips
1 yellow bell pepper, stemmed, quartered, seeded, and cut crosswise into ¼-inch-wide strips

Place a pizza brick, baking tiles, or a baking sheet in the oven and preheat the oven to 550°F.

Put the scallops in a nonreactive bowl. Toss the scallops with the olive oil, lemon juice, and herbs to coat the scallops well. Marinate at room temperature for about 15 minutes, turning the scallops two or three times.

Preheat the grill or broiler until very hot, with the cooking surface close to the heat. In four batches, sprinkle the scallops with salt and pepper to taste and grill or broil them for about 30 seconds per side, until just seared.

Place a ball of dough on a work surface sprinkled with semolina. Using the heels of your hands, press down to flatten the dough. Lift and gently pull the dough to stretch it into a circle 8 inches in diameter. With your fingertips, press and shape a ½-inch rim around the crust. Repeat with remaining balls of dough.

Spread ¼ cup of the sauce on each piece of dough up to the rim. Using about one-third of the mozzarella, sprinkle an equal amount on each pizza. Divide the scallops among the pizzas and scatter the pepper strips evenly over them. Top with the remaining cheese.

Carefully slide a pizza paddle under the pizzas, one at a time, and transfer them to the oven; with a slight push, slide each pizza off the paddle onto the baking surface. Bake the pizzas for 8 to 10 minutes or until the dough is browned and crisp and the cheese is golden and bubbly.

Serves 4

GRILLED SCALLOPS WITH PESTO, SUN-DRIED TOMATOES, AND FONTINA

Buy fresh sea scallops at least 1 inch in diameter; fresh-frozen scallops are also fine for this recipe. May also be made as a calzone (see page 23).

1 pound large sea scallops
3 tablespoons olive oil
1 tablespoon lemon juice
Salt and freshly ground black
  pepper
4 (6-ounce) balls pizza
  dough; use a Standard or

Sourdough Pizza Crust
(recipes on pages 14 and
16)
1 cup Pesto Sauce (recipe on
  page 20)
32 sun-dried tomato pieces
¾ pound fontina cheese

Place a pizza brick, baking tiles, or a baking sheet in the oven and preheat the oven to 550°F.

Put the scallops in a nonreactive bowl. Toss the scallops with the olive oil and lemon juice to coat the scallops well. Marinate at room temperature for about 15 minutes, turning the scallops two or three times.

Preheat the grill or broiler until very hot, with the cooking surface close to the heat. In four batches, sprinkle the scallops with salt and pepper to taste and grill or broil them for about 30 seconds per side, until just seared.

Place a ball of dough on a work surface sprinkled with semolina. Using the heels of your hands, press down to flatten the dough. Lift and gently pull the dough to stretch it into a circle 8 inches in diameter. With your fingertips, press and shape a ½-inch rim around the crust. Repeat with remaining balls of dough.

Spread ¼ cup of the sauce on each piece of dough up to the rim. Place sun-dried tomatoes on top of each pizza.

Using about a one-third of the fontina, pinch off small pieces of it with your fingers and distribute it equally over the four pizzas. Divide the scallops among the pizzas and dot the remaining cheese on top.

Carefully slide a pizza paddle under the pizzas, one at a time, and transfer them to the oven; with a slight push, slide each pizza off the paddle onto the baking surface. Bake the pizzas for 8 to 10 minutes or until the dough is browned and crisp and the cheese is golden and bubbly.

Serves 4

CRAB, PINE NUTS, ROASTED CHILIES, AND GOAT CHEESE

This pizza is inspired by a lunch dish at Saint Estephe restaurant in Manhattan Beach, California, where my friends chef John Sedlar and his partner Steve Garcia originated Modern Southwest Cuisine.

Try to buy flaked, cooked, fresh crabmeat at your local fish market. In a pinch, you can substitute canned crab. Whole canned Ortega chilies are a commercial brand of excellent quality, widely available in supermarkets.

May also be made as a calzone (see page 23).

4 (6-ounce) balls pizza dough; use a Standard Pizza Crust (recipe on page 14)

½ cup Pesto Sauce (recipe on page 20)

½ cup crème fraîche or heavy cream

4 whole canned Ortega chilies, torn into ¼-inch-wide strips

½ pound flaked crabmeat

6 ounces creamy goat cheese

¼ cup pine nuts

6 ounces mozzarella cheese, shredded

Place a pizza brick, baking tiles, or a baking sheet in the oven and preheat the oven to 550°F.

Place a ball of dough on a work surface sprinkled with semolina. Using the heels of your hands, press down to flatten the dough. Lift and gently pull the dough to stretch it into a circle 8 inches in diameter. With your fingertips, press and shape a ½-inch rim around the crust. Repeat with remaining balls of dough.

Stir together the sauce and crème fraîche. Spread one-quarter of the mixture on each piece of dough up to the rim. Scatter the chili strips over the pizzas.

With your fingertips, separate the crabmeat into flakes, removing any pieces of shell or gristle. Distribute the crab evenly over the pizzas.

With your fingertips, dot the goat cheese over the crab. Scatter the pine nuts on top, then cover each pizza with mozzarella.

Carefully slide a pizza paddle under the pizzas, one at a time, and transfer them to the oven; with a slight push, slide each pizza off the paddle onto the baking surface. Bake the pizzas for 8 to 10 minutes or until the dough is browned and crisp and the cheese is golden and bubbly.

Serves 4

CRAB WITH LEMON BUTTER AND FRESH MOZZARELLA

Lemon juice, orange and lemon zests, and mild, fresh mozzarella complement the sweet flavor of the crabmeat.

½ cup unsalted butter
2 tablespoons lemon juice
1 tablespoon grated lemon zest
½ tablespoon grated orange zest
½ teaspoon salt

4 (6-ounce) balls pizza dough; use a Standard Pizza Crust (recipe on page 14)
¾ pound fresh mozzarella cheese, thinly sliced
½ pound flaked crabmeat
¼ cup chopped fresh chives

Place a pizza brick, baking tiles, or a baking sheet in the oven and preheat the oven to 550°F.

Put the butter, lemon juice, citrus zests, and salt in a food processor fitted with the metal blade. Process continuously until smooth.

Place a ball of dough on a work surface sprinkled with semolina. Using the heels of your hands, press down to flatten the dough. Lift and gently pull the dough to stretch it into a circle 8 inches in diameter. With your fingertips, press and shape a ½-inch rim around the crust. Repeat with remaining balls of dough.

Spread one quarter of the butter mixture on each piece of dough up to the rim. Using about a quarter of the mozzarella slices, divide them evenly among the pizzas.

With your fingertips, separate the crabmeat into flakes, removing any pieces of shell or gristle. Distribute the crab evenly over the pizzas and sprinkle with the chives. Top pizzas with the remaining mozzarella slices.

Carefully slide a pizza paddle under the pizzas, one at a time, and transfer them to the oven; with a slight push, slide each pizza off the paddle onto the baking surface. Bake the pizzas for 8 to 10 minutes or until the dough is browned and crisp and the cheese is golden and bubbly.

Serves 4

CAVIAR AND CREME FRAICHE

Simplicity and elegance itself, this pizza makes a wonderful hors d'oeuvre served with dry champagne or iced vodka. American salmon caviar and golden caviar are relatively inexpensive and very delicious.

4 (6-ounce) balls pizza dough; use a Standard or Sourdough Pizza Crust (recipes on pages 14 and 16)

1 cup crème fraîche or sour cream
½ cup salmon caviar
½ cup golden caviar
¼ cup chopped fresh chives
1 lemon, cut into wedges

Place a pizza brick, baking tiles, or a baking sheet in the oven and preheat the oven to 550°F.

Place a ball of dough on a work surface sprinkled with semolina. Using the heels of your hands, press down to flatten the dough. Lift and gently pull the dough to stretch it into a circle 8 inches in diameter. With your fingertips, press and shape a ½-inch rim around the crust. Repeat with remaining balls of dough.

Carefully slide a pizza paddle under the pizzas, one at a time, and transfer them to the oven; with a slight push, slide each pizza off the paddle onto the baking surface. Bake the pizzas for 8 to 10 minutes or until the dough is browned and crisp.

Remove the pizzas from the oven and spread the crème fraîche or sour cream over the top of each. Cut the pizzas into wedges. With a teaspoon, distribute the salmon and golden caviar on the pizzas in a pattern that pleases you—concentric circles, alternating stripes, or a different caviar on alternating wedges. Scatter the chives on top and serve with lemon wedges.

Serves 4

CLAM AND GARLIC-HERB BUTTER

This is a classic seafood combination. Many seafood stores sell fresh baby clams already shelled. You can also use canned clams.

4 medium garlic cloves, peeled
½ cup unsalted butter
1½ tablespoons chopped fresh parsley
1½ tablespoons chopped fresh chives
½ teaspoon salt

4 (6-ounce) balls pizza dough; use a Standard or Sourdough Pizza Crust (recipes on pages 14 and 16)
½ pound shelled baby clams, drained
10 ounces mozzarella cheese, shredded

Place a pizza brick, baking tiles, or a baking sheet in the oven and preheat the oven to 550°F.

Put the garlic cloves in a food processor fitted with the metal blade. Turning the machine on and off rapidly, pulse the garlic until finely chopped. Add the butter, parsley, chives, and salt; process until smooth.

Place a ball of dough on a work surface sprinkled with semolina. Using the heels of your hands, press down to flatten the dough. Lift and gently pull the dough to stretch it into a circle 8 inches in diameter. With your fingertips, press and shape a ½-inch rim around the crust. Repeat with remaining balls of dough. Spread the garlic-herb butter up to the rim on each piece of dough.

Distribute an equal amount of the clams on top of the garlic-herb butter on each pizza. Sprinkle the mozzarella over the clams.

Carefully slide a pizza paddle under the pizzas, one at a time, and transfer them to the oven; with a slight push, slide each pizza off the paddle onto the baking surface. Bake the pizzas for 8 to 10 minutes or until the dough is browned and crisp and the cheese is golden and bubbly.

Serves 4

RED CLAM WITH FRESH GARLIC AND RED PEPPER

Crushed red pepper flakes give spark to this tomato-based clam topping. Fresh or canned clams work equally well.

4 (6-ounce) balls pizza dough; use a Standard or Sourdough Pizza Crust (recipes on pages 14 and 16)

1 cup Tomato Sauce (recipe on page 18)

6 medium garlic cloves, finely chopped

1½ teaspoons crushed red pepper flakes

¼ cup grated Parmesan cheese

½ pound shelled baby clams, drained

¼ pound provolone cheese, shredded

½ pound mozzarella cheese, shredded

Place a pizza brick, baking tiles, or a baking sheet in the oven and preheat the oven to 550°F.

Place a ball of dough on a work surface sprinkled with semolina. Using the heels of your hands, press down to flatten the dough. Lift and gently pull the dough to stretch it into a circle 8 inches in diameter. With your fingertips, press and shape a ½-inch rim around the crust. Repeat with remaining balls of dough.

Spread ¼ cup of the sauce on each piece of dough up to the rim. Sprinkle the red pepper flakes and garlic and then the Parmesan on each pizza.

Distribute an equal amount of the clams on top of each pizza. Sprinkle the provolone and mozzarella over the clams.

Carefully slide a pizza paddle under the pizzas, one at a time, and transfer them to the oven; with a slight push, slide each pizza off the paddle onto the baking surface. Bake the pizzas for 8 to 10 minutes or until the dough is browned and crisp and the cheese is golden and bubbly.

Serves 4

SMOKED OYSTERS WITH
PROVOLONE AND SMOKED MOZZARELLA

This is an intense pizza for those who love the smoky, briny flavor of smoked oysters. You'll find them near the anchovies or in the gourmet sections in most well-stocked supermarkets. Choose the smallest oysters, often labeled "petit." If you like, use regular mozzarella instead of smoked.

4 (6-ounce) balls pizza dough; use a Standard or Whole-Wheat Pizza Crust (recipes on pages 14 and 15)

1 cup Tomato Sauce (recipe on page 18)

¼ cup grated Parmesan cheese

2 3.66-ounce tins smoked oysters

6 ounces smoked mozzarella cheese, shredded

6 ounces provolone cheese, shredded

Place a pizza brick, baking tiles, or a baking sheet in the oven and preheat the oven to 550°F.

Place a ball of dough on a work surface sprinkled with semolina. Using the heels of your hands, press down to flatten the dough. Lift and gently pull the dough to stretch it into a circle 8 inches in diameter. With your fingertips, press and shape a ½-inch rim around the crust. Repeat with remaining balls of dough. Spread ¼ cup of the sauce on each piece of dough up to the rim. Then sprinkle the pizzas with the Parmesan.

Place an equal number of the smoked oysters on each pizza. With your fingertips, dot the smoked mozzarella over each pizza. Then sprinkle the provolone on top.

Carefully slide a pizza paddle under the pizzas, one at a time, and transfer them to the oven; with a slight push, slide each pizza off the paddle onto the baking surface. Bake the pizzas for 8 to 10 minutes or until the dough is browned and crisp and the cheese is golden and bubbly.

Serves 4

SMOKED SALMON, BOURSIN, CHIVES, AND SALMON CAVIAR

This is a perfect light luncheon or appetizer pizza. Boursin is widely available, as are other versions of cream cheese with garlic and herbs. Domestic salmon caviar provides a wonderfully elegant touch at a surprisingly reasonable cost.

4 (6-ounce) balls pizza dough; use a Standard Pizza Crust (recipe on page 14)

8 ounces Boursin cheese (French cream cheese with garlic and herbs), at room temperature

¾ pound smoked salmon, thinly sliced

1 (4-ounce) jar salmon caviar

¼ cup chopped fresh chives

1 lemon, cut into wedges

Place a pizza brick, baking tiles, or a baking sheet in the oven and preheat the oven to 550°F.

Place a ball of dough on a work surface sprinkled with semolina. Using the heels of your hands, press down to flatten the dough. Lift and gently pull the dough to stretch it into a circle 8 inches in diameter. With your fingertips, press and shape a ½-inch rim around the crust. Repeat with remaining balls of dough.

Spread one-quarter of the cheese on each piece of dough up to the rim.

Carefully slide a pizza paddle under the pizzas, one at a time, and transfer them to the oven; with a slight push, slide each pizza off the paddle onto the baking surface. Bake the pizzas for 8 to 10 minutes or until the dough is browned and crisp and the cheese is bubbly.

Remove the pizzas from the oven and lay the smoked salmon on top of each. Scatter the caviar and chives on top of each pizza and cut into wedges. Serve with lemon wedges. Squeeze over pizza to taste.

Serves 4

SMOKED SALMON WITH CREME FRAICHE, LEMON ZEST, AND CAPERS

Think of this as a sort of high-class, Sunday deli brunch pizza. If you can't get crème fraîche, substitute equal parts heavy cream and sour cream. Check your supermarket shelves for the smallest capers you can find.

4 (6-ounce) balls pizza
   dough; use a Standard or
   Sourdough Pizza Crust
   (recipes on pages 14 and 16)
1 cup crème fraîche
½ cup grated Parmesan
   cheese

¾ pound smoked salmon,
   thinly sliced
2 tablespoons lemon juice
4 teaspoons grated lemon
   zest
2½ tablespoons drained capers

Place a pizza brick, baking tiles, or a baking sheet in the oven and preheat the oven to 550°F.

Place a ball of dough on a work surface sprinkled with semolina. Using the heels of your hands, press down to flatten the dough. Lift and gently pull the dough to stretch it into a circle 8 inches in diameter. With your fingertips, press and shape a ½-inch rim around the crust. Repeat with remaining balls of dough. Spread ¼ cup of the crème fraîche on each piece of dough up to the rim. Sprinkle the Parmesan on each.

Carefully slide a pizza paddle under the pizzas, one at a time, and transfer them to the oven; with a slight push, slide each pizza off the paddle onto the baking surface. Bake the pizzas for 8 to 10 minutes or until the dough is browned and crisp and the topping is bubbly.

Remove the pizzas from the oven and lay the smoked salmon on top of each. Sprinkle with lemon juice and zest; top with the capers.

Serves 4

At right:
Asparagus Tips Alfredo (page 109)
On following page:
Fresh Mozzarella with Fresh Herbs (page 116)

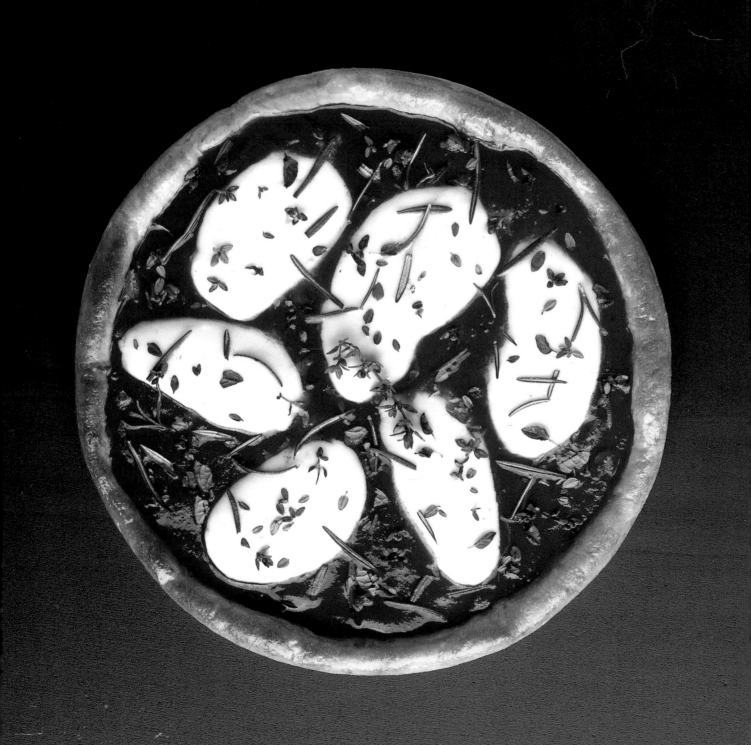

TUNA AND PROVOLONE

A confession: this pizza is an attempt to recapture one of the favorite dishes of my college years. At Broadway Pizza in New Haven, Connecticut, they make a hot tuna grinder that has achieved legendary status among Yale students. I've taken the same basic elements and turned them into a simple, satisfying pizza.

May also be made as a calzone (see page 23).

6 (3½-ounce) cans water-packed tuna
1 cup mayonnaise
2 tablespoons lemon juice
Salt and freshly ground black pepper
4 (6-ounce) balls pizza dough; use a Standard or

Sourdough Pizza Crust (recipes on pages 14 and 16)
1 pound provolone cheese, thinly sliced
2 ripe avocados, cut into thin wedges (optional)

Place a pizza brick, baking tiles, or a baking sheet in the oven and preheat the oven to 550°F.

In a nonreactive bowl, combine the tuna and its packing liquid with the mayonnaise and lemon juice. Mash well with a fork until the mixture is smooth. Season to taste with salt and a generous amount of black pepper.

Place a ball of dough on a work surface sprinkled with semolina. Using the heels of your hands, press down to flatten the dough. Lift and gently pull the dough to stretch it into a circle 8 inches in diameter. With your fingertips, press and shape a ½-inch rim around the crust. Repeat with remaining balls of dough.

Using half of the provolone slices, spread an equal portion over each piece of dough up to the rim.

Spread the tuna mixture on top of the cheese and place the remaining provolone slices over the tuna, covering it completely.

Carefully slide a pizza paddle under the pizzas, one at a time, and transfer them to the oven; with a slight push, slide each pizza off the paddle onto the baking surface. Bake the pizzas for 8 to 10 minutes or until the dough is browned and crisp and the cheese is golden and bubbly. If you like, arrange the avocado slices like the spokes of a wheel on top of each pizza.

Serves 4

ANCHOVIES AND GOLDEN ONIONS

This California-style pizza is a variation on the classic onion-and-anchovy-topped Provençale flat bread called pissaladiera. In this case, the topping is enhanced with sweet onions, which are caramelized in olive oil. Use Maui, Vidalia, or Walla Walla onions if they're available. If not, use the sweetest brown-skinned onions you can buy.

½ cup olive oil
2¾ pounds Maui onions,
   thinly sliced
Salt
4 (6-ounce) balls pizza
   dough; use a Standard or
   Sourdough Pizza Crust
   (recipes on pages 14 and 16)

½ cup grated Parmesan
   cheese
4 (2-ounce) tins anchovy
   fillets in olive oil, drained
6 ounces mozzarella cheese,
   shredded

Place a pizza brick, baking tiles, or a baking sheet in the oven and preheat the oven to 550°F.

In a large skillet, heat the olive oil over medium heat and add the onions and a sprinkling of salt. Sauté the onions, stirring frequently, until they turn golden, about 30 minutes. Adjust the heat lower so that the onions don't brown on the outside before their juices caramelize.

Place a ball of dough on a work surface sprinkled with semolina. Using the heels of your hands, press down to flatten the dough. Lift and gently pull the dough to stretch it into a circle 8 inches in diameter. With your fingertips, press and shape a ½-inch rim around the crust. Repeat with remaining balls of dough.

Spread one-quarter of the onions on each piece of dough up to the rim. Sprinkle Parmesan on top of each pizza. Then arrange a quarter of the anchovy fillets like the spokes of a wheel on top of each pizza. Top with the mozzarella.

Carefully slide a pizza paddle under the pizzas, one at a time, and transfer them to the oven; with a slight push, slide each pizza off the paddle onto the baking surface. Bake the pizzas for 8 to 10 minutes or until the dough is browned and crisp and the cheese is golden and bubbly.

Serves 4

ANCHOVIES, HERBS, AND RICOTTA

This pizza has the unmistakable flavor of the Mediterranean. Briny anchovies and aromatic herbs are contrasted by mild, fluffy ricotta.
May also be made as a calzone (see page 23).

4 (6-ounce) balls pizza dough; use a Standard or Whole-Wheat Pizza Crust (recipes on pages 14 and 15)
1 cup Tomato Sauce (recipe on page 18)
½ teaspoon dried oregano
½ teaspoon dried thyme
½ teaspoon dried rosemary
½ teaspoon dried savory
4 (2-ounce) tins anchovy fillets in olive oil, drained
10 ounces part-skim-milk ricotta cheese
6 ounces mozzarella cheese, shredded

Place a pizza brick, baking tiles, or a baking sheet in the oven and preheat the oven to 550°F.

Place a ball of dough on a work surface sprinkled with semolina. Using the heels of your hands, press down to flatten the dough. Lift and gently pull the dough to stretch it into a circle 8 inches in diameter. With your fingertips, press and shape a ½-inch rim around the crust. Repeat with remaining balls of dough.

Spread ¼ cup of the sauce on each piece of dough up to the rim. Sprinkle the herbs over the sauce on each. Then arrange the anchovy fillets like the spokes of a wheel on top of each pizza. Dot the ricotta on top, then cover each with the mozzarella.

Carefully slide a pizza paddle under the pizzas, one at a time, and transfer them to the oven; with a slight push, slide each pizza off the paddle onto the baking surface. Bake the pizzas for 8 to 10 minutes or until the dough is browned and crisp and the cheese is golden and bubbly.

Serves 4

ANCHOVIES WITH BLACK OLIVE PESTO

Anchovies and pungent, marinated black olives are frequent companions in Mediterranean cooking. Here the olives form a pestolike sauce that, combined with the salted fish, makes for a headily aromatic topping.

10 ounces medium-sized Niçoise olives (or other marinated black olives)

⅔ cup grated Parmesan cheese

⅔ cup olive oil

4 (6-ounce) balls pizza dough; use a Standard, Sourdough, or Whole-Wheat Pizza Crust (recipes on pages 14–16)

4 (2-ounce) tins anchovy fillets in olive oil, drained

10 ounces mozzarella cheese, shredded

Place a pizza brick, baking tiles, or a baking sheet in the oven and preheat the oven to 550°F.

Use your fingers to remove the olive pits. Put the olives, Parmesan, and olive oil in a food processor fitted with the metal blade. Process until pureed.

Place a ball of dough on a work surface sprinkled with semolina. Using the heels of your hands, press down to flatten the dough. Lift and gently pull the dough to stretch it into a circle 8 inches in diameter. With your fingertips, press and shape a ½-inch rim around the crust. Repeat with remaining balls of dough.

Spread the black olive puree up to the rim on each piece of dough. Then arrange the anchovy fillets like the spokes of a wheel on top of each pizza. Top each with the mozzarella.

Carefully slide a pizza paddle under the pizzas, one at a time, and transfer them to the oven; with a slight push, slide each pizza off the paddle onto the baking surface. Bake the pizzas for 8 to 10 minutes or until the dough is browned and crisp and the cheese is golden and bubbly.

Serves 4

ANCHOVIES, ROASTED GARLIC, AND THREE CHEESES

These pizzas are a real treat for lovers of anchovies and garlic. The Roasted Garlic Cloves temper the strength of the anchovies a bit; Pesto Sauce and three different cheeses add to the interplay of flavors.

4 (6-ounce) balls pizza dough; use a Standard, Sourdough, or Whole-Wheat Pizza Crust (recipes on pages 14–16)
1 cup Pesto Sauce (recipe on page 20)
32 medium Roasted Garlic Cloves (recipe on page 21)
½ cup grated Parmesan cheese
4 (2-ounce) tins anchovy fillets in olive oil, drained
6 ounces fontina cheese, shredded
¼ pound mozzarella cheese, shredded

Place a pizza brick, baking tiles, or a baking sheet in the oven and preheat the oven to 550°F.

Place a ball of dough on a work surface sprinkled with semolina. Using the heels of your hands, press down to flatten the dough. Lift and gently pull the dough to stretch it into a circle 8 inches in diameter. With your fingertips, press and shape a ½-inch rim around the crust. Repeat with remaining balls of dough.

Spread ¼ cup of the sauce on each piece of dough up to the rim. Distribute the Roasted Garlic Cloves over the pizzas, pressing down gently to spread them out. Sprinkle the Parmesan evenly over the sauce and garlic on each pizza.

Arrange the anchovy fillets like the spokes of a wheel on top of each pizza. Top each with the fontina and mozzarella.

Carefully slide a pizza paddle under the pizzas, one at a time, and transfer them to the oven; with a slight push, slide each pizza off the paddle onto the baking surface. Bake the pizzas for 8 to 10 minutes or until the dough is browned and crisp and the cheese is golden and bubbly.

Serves 4

6
VEGETABLE TOPPINGS

FRESH TOMATOES WITH PESTO AND GOAT CHEESE
TOMATO, BASIL, BUFFALO MOZZARELLA, AND OLIVE OIL
SUN-DRIED TOMATOES, PESTO, GOAT CHEESE, AND MOZZARELLA
SUN-DRIED TOMATOES, MASCARPONE, AND PINE NUTS
MARINATED OLIVES, PEPPERS, AND SUN-DRIED TOMATOES
MARINATED ARTICHOKES, RICOTTA, AND PARMESAN
HEARTS OF PALM, ARTICHOKE HEARTS, FONTINA, AND PESTO
ROASTED PEPPERS AND SMOKED MOZZARELLA
THREE MUSHROOMS AND THREE CHEESES
MUSHROOM AND GARLIC

ELEPHANT GARLIC, OLIVE OIL, AND OREGANO
SPINACH, ROASTED GARLIC, OLIVE OIL, AND RICOTTA
GRILLED JAPANESE EGGPLANT WITH GOAT CHEESE
MARINATED MAUI ONIONS WITH FOUR CHEESES
RED ONION WITH BARBECUE SAUCE AND SMOKED GOUDA
ASPARAGUS TIPS ALFREDO
GREEN AND YELLOW ZUCCHINI SAUTE WITH PERSILLADE AND GOAT CHEESE
PRIMAVERA WITH CREME FRAICHE
CALIFORNIA SPECIAL

FRESH TOMATOES WITH PESTO AND GOAT CHEESE

This is a simple, classic combination. Its success depends on using the best, firmest, most flavorful, in-season tomatoes you can find—preferably small Romas.
May also be made as a calzone (see page 23).

4 (6-ounce) balls pizza dough; use a Standard or Sourdough Pizza Crust (recipes on pages 14 and 16)

1 cup Pesto Sauce (recipe on page 20)

1 pound Roma tomatoes, stem ends removed and cut crosswise into ¼-inch-thick slices

½ pound fresh creamy goat cheese

6 ounces mozzarella cheese, shredded

Place a pizza brick, baking tiles, or a baking sheet in the oven and preheat the oven to 550°F.

Place a ball of dough on a work surface sprinkled with semolina. Using the heels of your hands, press down to flatten the dough. Lift and gently pull the dough to stretch it into a circle 8 inches in diameter. With your fingertips, press and shape a ½-inch rim around the crust. Repeat with remaining balls of dough.

Spread ¼ cup of the sauce on each piece of dough up to the rim. Place an equal number of tomato slices on top of the sauce on each pizza. Dot the goat cheese on top and cover each pizza with the mozzarella.

Carefully slide a pizza paddle under the pizzas one at a time, and transfer them to the oven; with a slight push, slide each pizza off the paddle onto the baking surface. Bake the pizzas for 8 to 10 minutes or until the dough is browned and crisp and the cheese is golden and bubbly.

Serves 4

TOMATO, BASIL, BUFFALO MOZZARELLA, AND OLIVE OIL

My wife describes this—and rightly so—as being just like eating a classic Italian salad on a pizza. If you can't get fresh mozzarella, by all means use your regular kind.

4 (6-ounce) balls pizza dough; use a Standard or Sourdough Pizza Crust (recipes on pages 14 and 16)

½ cup extra-virgin dark green olive oil

1 pound Roma tomatoes, stem ends removed and cut crosswise into ¼-inch-thick slices

Salt and freshly ground black pepper

24 large fresh basil leaves, rolled and cut crosswise into julienne strips

1 pound fresh buffalo mozzarella cheese, cut into ¼-inch-thick slices

Place a pizza brick, baking tiles, or baking sheet in the oven and preheat the oven to 550°F.

Place a ball of dough on a work surface sprinkled with semolina. Using the heels of your hands, press down to flatten the dough. Lift and gently pull the dough to stretch it into a circle 8 inches in diameter. With your fingertips, press and shape a ½-inch rim around the crust. Repeat with remaining balls of dough.

Spread one quarter of the olive oil on each piece of dough up to the rim. Distribute an equal number of the tomato slices on top of each pizza, turning them in the oil to coat the tomatoes on both sides. Sprinkle generously with salt and pepper to taste and scatter the basil on top of each pizza. Place the mozzarella slices over the tomato slices to cover them.

Carefully slide a pizza paddle under the pizzas, one at a time, and transfer them to the oven; with a slight push, slide each pizza off the paddle onto the baking surface. Bake the pizzas for 8 to 10 minutes or until the dough is browned and crisp and the cheese is golden and bubbly.

Serves 4

SUN-DRIED TOMATOES, PESTO, GOAT CHEESE, AND MOZZARELLA

Sun-dried tomatoes, popularized by California cooking, star in this combination of vivid tastes and colors.

May also be made as a calzone (see page 23).

4 (6-ounce) balls pizza dough; use a Standard or Sourdough Pizza Crust (recipes on pages 14 and 16)

1 cup Pesto Sauce (recipe on page 20)

6 ounces mozzarella cheese, shredded

40 sun-dried tomato pieces

½ pound fresh creamy goat cheese

Place a pizza brick, baking tiles, or a baking sheet in the oven and preheat the oven to 550°F.

Place a ball of dough on a work surface sprinkled with semolina. Using the heels of your hands, press down to flatten the dough. Lift and gently pull the dough to stretch it into a circle 8 inches in diameter. With your fingertips, press and shape a ½-inch rim around the crust. Repeat with remaining balls of dough.

Spread ¼ cup of the sauce on each piece of dough up to the rim. Sprinkle the mozzarella evenly over the sauce on each pizza. Place the sun-dried tomato pieces on top of each and dot the goat cheese evenly over the pizzas.

Carefully slide a pizza paddle under the pizzas, one at a time, and transfer them to the oven; with a slight push, slide each pizza off the paddle onto the baking surface. Bake the pizzas for 8 to 10 minutes or until the dough is browned and crisp and the cheese is golden and bubbly.

Serves 4

SUN-DRIED TOMATOES, MASCARPONE, AND PINE NUTS

Simple, intense flavors characterize this pizza. My brother-in-law Peter describes the overall effect as "elegant—like something you'd get from room service in a great hotel."

If you can't get mascarpone—the tangy Italian fresh cream cheese—use crème fraîche or equal parts of sour cream and heavy cream.

4 (6-ounce) balls pizza dough; use a Sourdough or Whole-Wheat Pizza Crust (recipes on pages 16 and 15)

1 cup mascarpone

½ cup grated Parmesan cheese

64 sun-dried tomato pieces

6 ounces mozzarella cheese, shredded

6 tablespoons pine nuts

Place a pizza brick, baking tiles, or a baking sheet in the oven and preheat the oven to 550°F.

Place a ball of dough on a work surface sprinkled with semolina. Using the heels of your hands, press down to flatten the dough. Lift and gently pull the dough to stretch it into a circle 8 inches in diameter. With your fingertips, press and shape a ½-inch rim around the crust. Repeat with remaining balls of dough.

Spread one-quarter of the mascarpone on each piece of dough up to the rim. Sprinkle the Parmesan over the mascarpone.

Distribute the sun-dried tomato pieces over the pizzas. Spread the mozzarella on top and sprinkle the pine nuts over the cheese.

Carefully slide a pizza paddle under the pizzas, one at a time, and transfer them to the oven; with a slight push, slide each pizza off the paddle onto the baking surface. Bake the pizzas for 8 to 10 minutes or until the dough is browned and crisp and the cheese is golden and bubbly.

Serves 4

MARINATED OLIVES, PEPPERS, AND SUN-DRIED TOMATOES

Seek out good, marinated, unpitted black olives at your local deli; Niçoise or Italian-style olives are a good bet. Likewise, buy a good jar of imported, marinated, roasted red bell peppers. Or roast your own and marinate them in equal parts olive oil and lemon juice with dried oregano, thyme, and rosemary. Then cover and refrigerate them.

4 (6-ounce) balls pizza dough; use a Standard or Sourdough Pizza Crust (recipes on pages 14 and 16)

1 cup Tomato Sauce (recipe on page 18)

32 marinated black olives, halved and pitted

2 medium red bell peppers, roasted (recipe on page 22) and marinated and torn into ¼-inch-wide strips

32 sun-dried tomato pieces

¼ pound provolone cheese, shredded

6 ounces mozzarella cheese, shredded

Place a pizza brick, baking tiles, or a baking sheet in the oven and preheat the oven to 550°F.

Place a ball of dough on a work surface sprinkled with semolina. Using the heels of your hands, press down to flatten the dough. Lift and gently pull the dough to stretch it into a circle 8 inches in diameter. With your fingertips, press and shape a ½-inch rim around the crust. Repeat with remaining balls of dough.

Spread ¼ cup of the sauce on each piece of dough up to the rim. Distribute the olive halves, peppers, and sun-dried tomatoes on top of the sauce on each pizza. Sprinkle the provolone over the vegetables and then distribute the mozzarella on top.

Carefully slide a pizza paddle under the pizzas, one at a time, and transfer them to the oven; with a slight push, slide each pizza off the paddle onto the baking surface. Bake the pizzas for 8 to 10 minutes or until the dough is browned and crisp and the cheese is golden and bubbly.

Serves 4

MARINATED ARTICHOKES, RICOTTA, AND PARMESAN

Buy good-quality marinated artichoke hearts for these pizzas. The ricotta makes a mild, fluffy background for the artichokes; the tang of the Parmesan provides sharp contrast.

May also be made as a calzone (see page 23).

4 (6-ounce) balls pizza dough; use a Sourdough or Whole-Wheat Pizza Crust (recipes on pages 16 and 15)

2 tablespoons mascarpone, crème fraîche, or equal parts heavy cream and sour cream

½ cup grated Parmesan cheese

12 marinated artichoke hearts, drained and quartered

1 cup (about 10 ounces) part-skim-milk ricotta cheese

6 ounces mozzarella cheese, shredded

Place a pizza brick, baking tiles, or a baking sheet in the oven and preheat the oven to 550°F.

Place a ball of dough on a work surface sprinkled with semolina. Using the heels of your hands, press down to flatten the dough. Lift and gently pull the dough to stretch it into a circle 8 inches in diameter. With your fingertips, press and shape a ½-inch rim around the crust. Repeat with remaining balls of dough.

Spread one-quarter of the mascarpone on each piece of dough up to the rim. Sprinkle the Parmesan on top of each.

Distribute the artichoke heart pieces over the pizzas. Dot the ricotta on top, then cover with the mozzarella.

Carefully slide a pizza paddle under the pizzas, one at a time, and transfer them to the oven; with a slight push, slide each pizza off the paddle onto the baking surface. Bake the pizzas for 8 to 10 minutes or until the dough is browned and crisp and the cheese is golden and bubbly.

Serves 4

HEARTS OF PALM, ARTICHOKE HEARTS, FONTINA, AND PESTO

Hunt down jars of marinated hearts of palm, which have more flavor than the canned variety. If you can get only canned, drain them well and cut them into 1-inch pieces. Then marinate them overnight, covered in the refrigerator, in equal parts of olive oil and good vinegar or lemon juice. Add a generous sprinkling of dried herbs—oregano, thyme, and rosemary.

4 (6-ounce) balls pizza dough; use a Standard, Sourdough, or Whole-Wheat Pizza Crust (recipes on pages 14–16)
1 cup Pesto Sauce (recipe on page 20)
½ cup grated Parmesan cheese
48 1-inch-long pieces marinated hearts of palm, drained
12 marinated artichoke hearts, drained and quartered
1 pound fontina cheese

Place a pizza brick, baking tiles, or a baking sheet in the oven and preheat the oven to 550°F.

Place a ball of dough on a work surface sprinkled with semolina. Using the heels of your hands, press down to flatten the dough. Lift and gently pull the dough to stretch it into a circle 8 inches in diameter. With your fingertips, press and shape a ½-inch rim around the crust. Repeat with remaining balls of dough.

Spread ¼ cup of the sauce on each piece of dough up to the rim. Sprinkle the Parmesan over the sauce.

Distribute the hearts of palm and artichoke hearts over each pizza. Dot the fontina on top.

Carefully slide a pizza paddle under the pizzas, one at a time, and transfer them to the oven; with a slight push, slide each pizza off the paddle onto the baking surface. Bake the pizzas for 8 to 10 minutes or until the dough is browned and crisp and the cheese is golden and bubbly.

Serves 4

ROASTED PEPPERS AND SMOKED MOZZARELLA

The smoky flavor of roasted peppers is perfectly partnered with smoked mozzarella cheese. If smoked mozzarella is unavailable, substitute equal parts of regular mozzarella and another smoked cheese such as gouda.
May also be made as a calzone (see page 23).

4 (6-ounce) balls pizza dough; use a Standard or Sourdough Pizza Crust (recipes on pages 14 and 16)

1 cup Pesto Sauce (recipe on page 20)

4 medium red bell peppers, roasted (recipe on page 22) and torn into ½-inch-wide strips

½ pound smoked mozzarella cheese

6 ounces mozzarella cheese, shredded

Place a pizza brick, baking tiles, or a baking sheet in the oven and preheat the oven to 550°F.

Place a ball of dough on a work surface sprinkled with semolina. Using the heels of your hands, press down to flatten the dough. Lift and gently pull the dough to stretch it into a circle 8 inches in diameter. With your fingertips, press and shape a ½-inch rim around the crust. Repeat with remaining balls of dough.

Spread ¼ cup of the sauce on each piece of dough up to the rim. Arrange the pepper strips on top of the pizzas. Pinch off pieces of the smoked mozzarella with your fingertips and dot them on top of the pizzas. Sprinkle the mozzarella on top of each.

Carefully slide a pizza paddle under the pizzas, one at a time, and transfer them to the oven; with a slight push, slide each pizza off the paddle onto the baking surface. Bake the pizzas for 8 to 10 minutes or until the dough is browned and crisp and the cheese is golden and bubbly.

Serves 4

THREE MUSHROOMS AND THREE CHEESES

One byproduct of the California culinary revolution is the wide variety of fresh mushrooms now available in many of our supermarkets. This pizza uses standard fresh button mushrooms—themselves a California innovation in the late 1950s— along with pale grey, tender oyster mushrooms and thin, pale enoki mushrooms.

If you can't find the latter two varieties, use whatever fresh mushrooms are available. In a pinch, make the pizza solely with button mushrooms.

4 (6-ounce) balls pizza dough; use a Standard or Whole-Wheat Pizza Crust (recipes on pages 14–15)

1 cup Pesto Sauce (recipe on page 20)

½ pound button mushrooms, cut crosswise into ¼-inch-thick slices

½ cup grated Parmesan cheese

6 ounces mozzarella cheese, shredded

6 ounces fresh medium-sized oyster mushrooms

¼ pound fresh enoki mushrooms

6 ounces fontina cheese, shredded

Place a pizza brick, baking tiles, or a baking sheet in the oven and preheat the oven to 550°F.

Place a ball of dough on a work surface sprinkled with semolina. Using the heels of your hands, press down to flatten the dough. Lift and gently pull the dough to stretch it into a circle 8 inches in diameter. With your fingertips, press and shape a ½-inch rim around the crust. Repeat with remaining balls of dough. Spread ¼ cup of the sauce on each piece of dough up to the rim.

Distribute the button mushroom slices over the pizzas. Sprinkle with the Parmesan and spread the mozzarella on top of each pizza. Place the whole oyster mushrooms on top of the mozzarella, interspersed with small clusters of enoki mushrooms. Spread the fontina over the pizzas.

Carefully slide a pizza paddle under the pizzas, one at a time, and transfer them to the oven; with a slight push, slide each pizza off the paddle onto the baking surface. Bake the pizzas for 8 to 10 minutes or until the dough is browned and crisp and the cheese is golden and bubbly.

Serves 4

MUSHROOM AND GARLIC

Chopped mushrooms and garlic cook down to an intensely flavored topping for pizzas so that they need no sauce. This is a real mushroom-lover's pizza.

½ cup unsalted butter
8 medium garlic cloves, finely chopped
1¾ pounds button mushrooms, coarsely chopped
Salt and freshly ground black pepper
¼ cup chopped fresh parsley
½ cup heavy cream

4 (6-ounce) balls pizza dough; use a Whole-Wheat Pizza Crust (recipe on page 15)
1 cup grated Parmesan cheese
6 ounces provolone cheese, shredded
6 ounces mozzarella cheese, shredded

Place a pizza brick, baking tiles, or a baking sheet in the oven and preheat the oven to 550°F.

In a large skillet, melt the butter over medium heat. Add the garlic and sauté about 1 minute. Then add the mushrooms and season with salt and generous grindings of pepper. Sauté the mushrooms, stirring frequently, until all their liquid has evaporated and they begin to turn golden, 15 to 20 minutes.

Stir in the parsley, then add the cream and stir briefly just until it has been absorbed by the mushrooms. Empty the mushroom mixture into a bowl and let it cool for about 10 minutes, stirring occasionally.

Place a ball of dough on a work surface sprinkled with semolina. Using the heels of your hands, press down to flatten the dough. Lift and gently pull the dough to stretch it into a circle 8 inches in diameter. With your fingertips, press and shape a ½-inch rim around the crust. Repeat with remaining balls of dough. Spread ¼ cup of the sauce on each piece of dough up to the rim. Sprinkle the Parmesan, provolone, and mozzarella on top of each pizza.

Carefully slide a pizza paddle under the pizzas, one at a time, and transfer them to the oven; with a slight push, slide each pizza off the paddle onto the baking surface. Bake the pizzas for 8 to 10 minutes or until the dough is browned and crisp and the cheese is golden and bubbly.

Serves 4

ELEPHANT GARLIC, OLIVE OIL, AND OREGANO

Mammoth cloves of sweet, mild elephant garlic are an increasingly popular element of California cooking. Elephant garlic possesses the flavor of conventional garlic without the assertiveness.

4 (6 ounce) balls pizza dough; use a Standard or Sourdough Pizza Crust (recipes on pages 14 and 16)

½ cup olive oil

¾ cup grated Parmesan cheese

½ cup grated pecorino cheese

12 cloves elephant garlic, peeled and thinly sliced

½ pound mozzarella cheese, shredded

Place a pizza brick, baking tiles, or a baking sheet in the oven and preheat the oven to 550°F.

Place a ball of dough on a work surface sprinkled with semolina. Using the heels of your hands, press down to flatten the dough. Lift and gently pull the dough to stretch it into a circle 8 inches in diameter. With your fingertips, press and shape a ½-inch rim around the crust. Repeat with remaining balls of dough. Spread one quarter of the oil on each piece of dough up to the rim. Sprinkle the Parmesan and pecorino cheese over the oil on each.

Distribute the elephant garlic slices evenly over the pizza. Top with the mozzarella.

Carefully slide a pizza paddle under the pizzas, one at a time, and transfer them to the oven; with a slight push, slide each pizza off the paddle onto the baking surface. Bake the pizzas for 8 to 10 minutes or until the dough is browned and crisp and the cheese is golden and bubbly.

Serves 4

SPINACH, ROASTED GARLIC, OLIVE OIL, AND RICOTTA

Spinach and garlic, classic companions, join together in this simple, elegant pizza. May also be made as a calzone (see page 23).

4 (6 ounce) balls pizza dough; use a Standard, Sourdough, or Whole-Wheat Pizza Crust (recipes on pages 14–16)

⅓ cup olive oil from Roasted Garlic Cloves

32 medium Roasted Garlic Cloves (recipe on page 21)

¾ cup grated Parmesan cheese

¼ pound mozzarella cheese, shredded

32 medium spinach leaves, thoroughly washed, dried, stemmed, ribbed, and cut crosswise into ¼-inch-wide strips

½ pound part-skim-milk ricotta cheese

¼ pound fontina cheese, shredded

Place a pizza brick, baking tiles, or a baking sheet in the oven and preheat the oven to 550°F.

Place a ball of dough on a work surface sprinkled with semolina. Using the heels of your hands, press down to flatten the dough. Lift and gently pull the dough to stretch it into a circle 8 inches in diameter. With your fingertips, press and shape a ½-inch rim around the crust. Repeat with remaining balls of dough.

Spread one quarter cup of the oil on each piece of dough up to the rim. Place the Roasted Garlic Cloves on top, gently pressing down to spread them. Sprinkle the Parmesan and mozzarella evenly over the garlic and oil on each pizza.

Spread the spinach leaves evenly over each pizza. Dot the ricotta on top and then spread the fontina over each.

Carefully slide a pizza paddle under the pizzas, one at a time, and transfer them to the oven; with a slight push, slide each pizza off the paddle onto the baking surface. Bake the pizzas for 8 to 10 minutes or until the dough is browned and crisp and the cheese is golden and bubbly.

Serves 4

GRILLED JAPANESE EGGPLANT WITH GOAT CHEESE

Small, slender Japanese eggplants have a finer flavor and fewer, smaller seeds than the large varieties. If your local market doesn't have them, buy the smallest eggplants you can find. May also be made as a calzone (see page 23).

1 pound Japanese eggplant, stemmed, flower ends trimmed, peeled, and cut lengthwise into ¼-inch-thick slices

6 tablespoons olive oil

Salt and freshly ground black pepper

4 (6 ounce) balls pizza dough; use a Standard, Sourdough, or Whole-Wheat Pizza Crust (recipes on pages 14–16)

1 cup Tomato Sauce (recipe on page 18)

½ cup grated Parmesan cheese

6 ounces fresh creamy goat cheese

6 ounces Mozzarella cheese, shredded

Place a pizza brick, baking tiles, or a baking sheet in the oven and preheat the oven to 550°F.

Preheat the grill or broiler until very hot, with the cooking surface close to the heat. Brush the eggplant slices on both sides with the olive oil and sprinkle them with salt and pepper. Grill or broil the eggplant until seared and partially cooked, 1 to 1½ minutes per side. Set aside.

Place a ball of dough on a work surface sprinkled with semolina. Using the heels of your hands, press down to flatten the dough. Lift and gently pull the dough to stretch it into a circle 8 inches in diameter. With your fingertips, press and shape a ½-inch rim around the crust. Repeat with remaining balls of dough.

Spread ¼ cup of the sauce on each piece of dough up to the rim. Sprinkle each pizza with Parmesan. Place the eggplant slices on top of the pizzas. Dot the goat cheese on top and cover with the mozzarella.

Carefully slide a pizza paddle under the pizzas, one at a time, and transfer them to the oven; with a slight push, slide each pizza off the paddle onto the baking surface. Bake the pizzas for 8 to 10 minutes or until the dough is browned and crisp and the cheese is golden and bubbly.

Serves 4

MARINATED MAUI ONIONS WITH FOUR CHEESES

Briefly marinated with mellow balsamic vinegar and herbs, sweet Maui onions develop a fabulous flavor that is shown off in this pizza.

3 cups thinly sliced Maui onions

½ cup olive oil

3 tablespoons balsamic vinegar

1½ teaspoons dried oregano

½ teaspoon dried thyme

½ teaspoon dried rosemary

½ teaspoon dried savory

¼ teaspoon salt

¼ teaspoon freshly ground black pepper

4 (6 ounce) balls pizza dough; use a Standard, Sourdough, or Whole-Wheat Pizza Crust (recipes on pages 14–16)

¾ pound mozzarella cheese, shredded

½ cup grated Parmesan cheese

¼ cup grated Romano cheese

¼ cup grated pecorino cheese

In a mixing bowl, toss the onions with the oil, vinegar, herbs, salt, and pepper. Cover with plastic wrap and marinate at room temperature for 30 minutes to 1 hour.

Place a pizza brick, baking tiles, or a baking sheet in the oven and preheat the oven to 550°F.

Place a ball of dough on a work surface sprinkled with semolina. Using the heels of your hands, press down to flatten the dough. Lift and gently pull the dough to stretch it into a circle 8 inches in diameter. With your fingertips, press and shape a ½-inch rim around the crust. Repeat with remaining balls of dough.

Using half of the mozzarella, spread an equal portion of it on each piece of dough up to the rim. Top each crust with the onion mixture. Sprinkle the Parmesan, Romano, and pecorino cheeses over the onion mixture on each pizza. Top with the remaining mozzarella.

Carefully slide a pizza paddle under the pizzas, one at a time, and transfer them to the oven; with a slight push, slide each pizza off the paddle onto the baking surface. Bake the pizzas for 8 to 10 minutes or until the dough is browned and crisp and the cheese is golden and bubbly.

Serves 4

RED ONION WITH BARBECUE SAUCE AND SMOKED GOUDA

Here's a vegetarian version of the barbecue-flavored pizzas popular in many California-styled pizzerias.

4 (6 ounce) balls pizza dough; use a Standard, Sourdough, or Whole-Wheat Pizza Crust (recipes on pages 14–16)

1 cup Barbecue Sauce (recipe on page 19)

6 ounces mozzarella cheese, shredded

1½ cups thinly sliced red onions

6 ounces smoked Gouda cheese, shredded

Place a pizza brick, baking tiles, or a baking sheet in the oven and preheat the oven to 550°F.

Place a ball of dough on a work surface sprinkled with semolina. Using the heels of your hands, press down to flatten the dough. Lift and gently pull the dough to stretch it into a circle 8 inches in diameter. With your fingertips, press and shape a ½-inch rim around the crust. Repeat with remaining balls of dough.

Spread ¼ cup of the sauce on each piece of dough up to the rim. Using half of the mozzarella, sprinkle an equal portion of it on each pizza. Spread the onions on top, then the remaining mozzarella and the smoked Gouda.

Carefully slide a pizza paddle under the pizzas, one at a time, and transfer them to the oven; with a slight push, slide each pizza off the paddle onto the baking surface. Bake the pizzas for 8 to 10 minutes or until the dough is browned and crisp and the cheese is golden and bubbly.

Serves 4

ASPARAGUS TIPS ALFREDO

A thick cheese sauce, similar to the classic Italian Alfredo sauce, envelopes spears of asparagus on this elegant pizza.

1½ cups heavy cream
5 ounces Romano cheese, grated
4 ounces Parmesan cheese, grated
2 dozen asparagus spears, trimmed to 4-inch tips

4 (6 ounce) balls pizza dough; use a Standard or Sourdough Pizza Crust (recipes on pages 14 and 16)
Freshly ground black pepper

Place a pizza brick, baking tiles, or a baking sheet in the oven and preheat the oven to 550°F.

Meanwhile, bring the cream to a boil over high heat in a heavy saucepan. Reduce the heat to a bare simmer and slowly stir in the Romano and Parmesan. Continue simmering, stirring frequently, until the sauce is very thick, about 10 minutes. Remove from the heat.

Bring a separate pan of lightly salted water to a boil. Add the asparagus and boil for 30 seconds. Immediately drain and rinse the asparagus under cold running water until cool. Drain and pat the asparagus dry.

Place a ball of dough on a work surface sprinkled with semolina. Using the heels of your hands, press down to flatten the dough. Lift and gently pull the dough to stretch it into a circle 8 inches in diameter. With your fingertips, press and shape a ½-inch rim around the crust. Repeat with remaining balls of dough.

Using half the cheese sauce, spread an equal portion of it on each piece of dough up to the rim. Season generously with black pepper. Place the asparagus tips on each pizza like spokes of a wheel, with the tips slightly overlapping the rim. Spoon the remaining sauce over the asparagus, leaving the very ends of the tips uncovered.

Carefully slide a pizza paddle under the pizzas, one at a time, and transfer them to the oven; with a slight push, slide each pizza off the paddle onto the baking surface. Bake the pizzas for 8 to 10 minutes or until the dough is browned and crisp and the cheese is golden and bubbly.

Serves 4

GREEN AND YELLOW ZUCCHINI SAUTE WITH PERSILLADE AND GOAT CHEESE

Strands of green and yellow zucchini, sautéed in olive oil, make an excellent pizza topping without sauce. If yellow zucchini isn't available, use small yellow summer squash or all green zucchini.

¾ pound green zucchini
¾ pound yellow zucchini
1½ teaspoons salt
½ cup olive oil
6 medium garlic cloves, finely chopped
6 tablespoons chopped fresh parsley

4 (6 ounce) balls pizza dough; use a Standard or Whole-Wheat Pizza Crust (recipes on pages 14–15)
½ pound mozzarella cheese
½ cup grated Parmesan cheese
¾ pound fresh creamy goat cheese

Place a pizza brick, baking tiles, or a baking sheet in the oven and preheat the oven to 550°F.

With a food processor or hand grater, finely shred the zucchini. In a mixing bowl, toss the zucchini with the salt, mixing them well. Let the zucchini stand for about 10 minutes. Then pick up small handfuls and, working over the sink, squeeze the zucchini tightly to extract as much liquid as possible. (Much of the salt will go down the drain with the liquid.)

In a large skillet, heat the olive oil over moderate-to-high heat. Add the zucchini and cook, stirring constantly, for about 4 minutes. Remove from the heat, toss with the garlic and parsley; let cool.

Place a ball of dough on a work surface sprinkled with semolina. Using the heels of your hands, press down to flatten the dough. Lift and gently pull the dough to stretch it into a circle 8 inches in diameter. With your fingertips, press and shape a ½-inch rim around the crust. Repeat with remaining balls of dough.

Using about one third of the mozzarella, spread an equal portion of it on the four crusts up to the rim. Then spread the zucchini mixture up to the rim on each piece of dough. Sprinkle each with the Parmesan, then dot the goat cheese on top. Sprinkle a portion of the remaining mozzarella over each pizza.

Carefully slide a pizza paddle under the pizzas, one at a time, and transfer them to the oven; with a slight push, slide each pizza off the paddle onto the baking surface. Bake the pizzas for 8 to 10 minutes or until the dough is browned and crisp and the cheese is golden and bubbly.

Serves 4

PRIMAVERA WITH CREME FRAICHE

Primavera is Italian for springtime, and this pizza is topped with a spring harvest of vegetables. For the most beautiful presentation, seek out baby vegetables from a gourmet-quality greengrocer. If baby vegetables are unavailable, use the smallest, most tender vegetables you can find.

4 (6 ounce) balls pizza dough; use a Standard or Sourdough Pizza Crust (recipes on pages 14 and 16)
1 cup crème fraîche
½ cup grated Parmesan cheese
¼ pound provolone cheese, shredded
¾ cup thinly sliced red onion
¼ pound baby zucchini, trimmed and very thinly sliced crosswise at a 45-degree angle

¼ pound baby yellow squash, trimmed and very thinly sliced crosswise at a 45-degree angle
¼ pound baby carrots, trimmed and very thinly sliced crosswise at a 45-degree angle
¼ pound small broccoli florets
10 ounces mozzarella cheese, shredded

Place a pizza brick, baking tiles, or a baking sheet in the oven and preheat the oven to 550°F.

Place a ball of dough on a work surface sprinkled with semolina. Using the heels of your hands, press down to flatten the dough. Lift and gently pull the dough to stretch it into a circle 8 inches in diameter. With your fingertips, press and shape a ½-inch rim around the crust. Repeat with remaining balls of dough.

Spread ¼ cup of the crème fraîche on each piece of dough up to the rim. Sprinkle the Parmesan on top of each, then sprinkle on the provolone. Scatter the onions over the cheese. Arrange zucchini, squash, carrot slices, and broccoli in a decorative pattern on each pizza. Sprinkle mozzarella on top.

Carefully slide a pizza paddle under the pizzas, one at a time, and transfer them to the oven; with a slight push, slide each pizza off the paddle onto the baking surface. Bake the pizzas for 8 to 10 minutes or until the dough is browned and crisp and the cheese is golden and bubbly.

Serves 4

CALIFORNIA SPECIAL

Goat cheese, avocado, and alfalfa sprouts have been used with such indiscriminate abandon in California cooking that they have become clichés. Nevertheless, they're a wonderful topping for a light, luncheon-style pizza.

4 (6 ounce) balls pizza dough; use a Standard, Sourdough, or Whole-Wheat Pizza Crust (recipes on pages 14–16)
¼ cup olive oil

1 pound fresh creamy goat cheese
Freshly ground black pepper
2 medium-sized ripe avocados
2 ounces alfalfa sprouts
2 tablespoons lemon juice

Place a pizza brick, baking tiles, or a baking sheet in the oven and preheat the oven to 550°F.

Place a ball of dough on a work surface sprinkled with semolina. Using the heels of your hands, press down to flatten the dough. Lift and gently pull the dough to stretch it into a circle 8 inches in diameter. With your fingertips, press and shape a ½-inch rim around the crust. Repeat with remaining balls of dough.

Spread one-quarter of the olive oil on each piece of dough up to the rim. Dot the goat cheese over each pizza and season generously with black pepper.

Carefully slide a pizza paddle under the pizzas, one at a time, and transfer them to the oven; with a slight push, slide each pizza off the paddle onto the baking surface. Bake the pizzas for 8 to 10 minutes or until the dough is browned and crisp and the cheese is golden and bubbly.

Meanwhile, halve, pit, and peel the avocados; cut each lengthwise into 12 slices. When the pizzas are baked, arrange the avocado slices on top of each. Top with alfalfa sprouts. Sprinkle with lemon juice

Serves 4

7
CHEESE TOPPINGS

FRESH MOZZARELLA WITH FRESH HERBS
RICOTTA WITH ROASTED GARLIC AND PESTO
QUESO FUNDIDO
MARINATED GOAT CHEESE
FETA WITH GREEK OLIVE PESTO
GORGONZOLA AND MASCARPONE WITH PINE NUTS

STILTON AND WALNUT
BRIE AND ALMOND WITH MUSTARD SAUCE
SMOKED CHEDDAR WITH BARBECUE SAUCE
SMOKED CHEESE MEDLEY WITH CREME FRAICHE
FONTINA, GOAT CHEESE, PARMESAN, AND MOZZARELLA

FRESH MOZZARELLA WITH FRESH HERBS

In this recipe, the classic cheese and tomato pizza is refined to the ultimate elegance. Of course, if you can't find fresh mozzarella, substitute the best regular mozzarella you can buy.

4 **(6-ounce) balls pizza dough; use a Standard or Sourdough Pizza Crust (recipes on pages 14 and 16)**

1 **cup Tomato Sauce (recipe on page 18)**

1½ **tablespoons chopped fresh oregano leaves**

1 **teaspoon chopped fresh thyme leaves**

1 **teaspoon chopped fresh rosemary leaves**

1 **pound fresh buffalo mozzarella, cut into ¼-inch-thick slices**

Place a pizza brick, baking tiles, or a baking sheet in the oven and preheat the oven to 550°F.

Place a ball of dough on a work surface sprinkled with semolina. Using the heels of your hands, press down to flatten the dough. Lift and gently pull the dough to stretch it into a circle 8 inches in diameter. With your fingertips, press and shape a ½-inch rim around the crust. Repeat with remaining balls of dough.

Spread ¼ cup of the sauce on each piece of dough up to the rim. Sprinkle the herbs over the sauce. Place the mozzarella slices on top of each pizza.

Carefully slide a pizza paddle under the pizzas and transfer them to the oven; with a slight push, slide each pizza off the paddle onto the baking surface. Bake the pizzas for 8 to 10 minutes or until the dough is browned and crisp and the cheese is golden and bubbly.

Serves 4

RICOTTA WITH ROASTED GARLIC AND PESTO

A study in mellow flavors—sweet, creamy ricotta and mellow Roasted Garlic Cloves. May also be made as a calzone (see page 23).

4 (6-ounce) balls pizza dough; use a Standard, Sourdough, or Whole-Wheat Pizza Crust (recipes on pages 14–16)
1 cup Pesto Sauce (recipe on page 20)

24 medium Roasted Garlic Cloves (recipe on page 21)
½ cup grated Parmesan cheese
½ pound part-skim-milk ricotta cheese
6 ounces mozzarella cheese, shredded

Place a pizza brick, baking tiles, or a baking sheet in the oven and preheat the oven to 550°F.

Place a ball of dough on a work surface sprinkled with semolina. Using the heels of your hands, press down to flatten the dough. Lift and gently pull the dough to stretch it into a circle 8 inches in diameter. With your fingertips, press and shape a ½-inch rim around the crust. Repeat with remaining balls of dough.

Spread ¼ cup of the sauce on each piece of dough up to the rim. Place the Roasted Garlic Cloves on top of the pizzas, gently pressing the cloves down to spread them. Sprinkle the Parmesan over the sauce and garlic. Dot the ricotta evenly on top of the pizzas. Then sprinkle with the mozzarella.

Carefully slide a pizza paddle under the pizzas, one at a time, and transfer them to the oven; with a slight push, slide each pizza off the paddle onto the baking surface. Bake the pizzas for 8 to 10 minutes or until the dough is browned and crisp and the cheese is golden and bubbly.

Serves 4

QUESO FUNDIDO

Mexican "melted cheese" is a popular appetizer in Cal-Mex restaurants. It's a mixture of Monterey Jack—which was developed in Monterey County during the nineteenth century by Scotsman David Jacks—and green chilies. Here it is refined into a pizza topping.

May also be made as a calzone (see page 23).

4 (6-ounce) balls pizza dough; use a Standard or Sourdough Pizza Crust (recipes on pages 14 and 16)

1 cup crème fraîche, mascarpone, or heavy cream

½ cup grated Parmesan cheese

4 whole canned Ortega chilies, torn into ¼-inch-wide strips

¾ pound Monterey Jack cheese, shredded

Place a pizza brick, baking tiles, or a baking sheet in the oven and preheat the oven to 550°F.

Place a ball of dough on a work surface sprinkled with semolina. Using the heels of your hands, press down to flatten the dough. Lift and gently pull the dough to stretch it into a circle 8 inches in diameter. With your fingertips, press and shape a ½-inch rim around the crust. Repeat with remaining balls of dough.

Spread ¼ cup of the crème fraîche on each piece of dough up to the rim. Sprinkle the Parmesan over the crème fraîche. Scatter the chili strips on top, then sprinkle evenly with the Monterey Jack.

Carefully slide a pizza paddle under the pizzas, one at a time, and transfer them to the oven; with a slight push, slide each pizza off the paddle onto the baking surface. Bake the pizzas for 8 to 10 minutes or until the dough is browned and crisp and the cheese is golden and bubbly.

Serves 4

MARINATED GOAT CHEESE

A Northern California culinary entrepreneur named Laura Chenel is now making the best goat cheese in the country. In fact, her cheese ranks with the best in the world. One of her finest products is little rounds of creamy goat cheese, called "cabecou," marinated in olive oil and herbs.

Her products are marketed nationwide, and you can also order them by mail, writing to her company at 1908 Innes Street, San Francisco, California 94124, or phoning (415) 648-5252.

There are many other fine goat cheesemakers around the country and, if you can't find Chenel's product, chances are you'll find some similar herb-marinated goat cheese in your local gourmet market.

May also be made as a calzone (see page 23).

4 (6-ounce) balls pizza dough; use a Standard, Sourdough, or Whole-Wheat Pizza Crust (recipes on pages 14–16)

1 cup Tomato Sauce (recipe on page 18)
¾ pound marinated goat cheese
6 ounces mozzarella cheese, shredded

Place a pizza brick, baking tiles, or a baking sheet in the oven and preheat the oven to 550°F.

Place a ball of dough on a work surface sprinkled with semolina. Using the heels of your hands, press down to flatten the dough. Lift and gently pull the dough to stretch it into a circle 8 inches in diameter. With your fingertips, press and shape a ½-inch rim around the crust. Repeat with remaining balls of dough.

Spread ¼ cup of the sauce on each piece of dough up to the rim. Dot the goat cheese evenly on top of each pizza. Then sprinkle evenly with the mozzarella.

Carefully slide a pizza paddle under the pizzas, one at a time, and transfer them to the oven; with a slight push, slide each pizza off the paddle onto the baking surface. Bake the pizzas for 8 to 10 minutes or until the dough is browned and crisp and the cheese is golden and bubbly.

Serves 4

FETA WITH GREEK OLIVE PESTO

Briny, grey-black marinated Greek olives are the basis of a sauce that complements a topping of Greek goat cheese—feta.

10 ounces medium-sized unpitted Greek olives (or other marinated black olives)
24 sun-dried tomato pieces
½ cup olive oil
2 tablespoons lemon juice

4 (6-ounce) balls pizza dough; use a Standard or Sourdough Pizza Crust (recipes on pages 14 and 16)
½ pound feta cheese
½ pound mozzarella cheese, shredded

Place a pizza brick, baking tiles, or a baking sheet in the oven and preheat the oven to 550°F.

With your fingers, remove and discard the olive pits. Put the olives, sun-dried tomatoes, olive oil, and lemon juice in a food processor fitted with the metal blade and process until the mixture is pureed.

Place a ball of dough on a work surface sprinkled with semolina. Using the heels of your hands, press down to flatten the dough. Lift and gently pull the dough to stretch it into a circle 8 inches in diameter. With your fingertips, press and shape a ½-inch rim around the crust. Repeat with remaining balls of dough.

Spread one quarter of the olive puree on each piece of dough up to the rim. Crumble the feta over the sauce on each pizza. Sprinkle the mozzarella evenly on top of each.

Carefully slide a pizza paddle under the pizzas, and transfer them to the oven; with a slight push, slide each pizza off the paddle onto the baking surface. Bake the pizzas for 8 to 10 minutes or until the dough is browned and crisp and the cheese is golden and bubbly.

Serves 4

GORGONZOLA AND MASCARPONE WITH PINE NUTS

The tangy Italian blue cheese, gorgonzola, meets its match in the creamy, tangy mascarpone that serves as the sauce here. If you can't find gorgonzola, substitute whatever good blue cheese is available; likewise, substitute crème fraîche or heavy cream for the mascarpone, if necessary.

May also be made as a calzone (see page 23).

4 (6-ounce) balls pizza dough; use a Standard or Sourdough Pizza Crust (recipes on pages 14 and 16)

1 cup mascarpone, crème fraîche, or heavy cream
10 ounces gorgonzola cheese
6 tablespoons pine nuts
6 ounces mozzarella cheese, shredded

Place a pizza brick, baking tiles, or a baking sheet in the oven and preheat the oven to 550°F.

Place a ball of dough on a work surface sprinkled with semolina. Using the heels of your hands, press down to flatten the dough. Lift and gently pull the dough to stretch it into a circle 8 inches in diameter. With your fingertips, press and shape a ½-inch rim around the crust. Repeat with remaining balls of dough.

Spread ¼ cup of the mascarpone on each piece of dough up to the rim. Dot the gorgonzola evenly over the pizzas and sprinkle them with pine nuts. Then top with the mozzarella.

Carefully slide a pizza paddle under the pizzas, one at a time, and transfer them to the oven; with a slight push, slide each pizza off the paddle onto the baking surface. Bake the pizzas for 8 to 10 minutes or until the dough is browned and crisp and the cheese is golden and bubbly.

Serves 4

STILTON AND WALNUT

This is a classic English combination, perfect to serve for a luncheon or to use as an hors d'oeuvre.

4 (6-ounce) balls pizza dough; use a Standard or Whole-Wheat Pizza Crust (recipes on pages 14-15)
1 cup heavy cream

10 ounces stilton or other blue cheese
6 tablespoons walnut pieces
6 ounces mozzarella cheese, shredded

Place a pizza brick, baking tiles, or a baking sheet in the oven and preheat the oven to 550°F.

Place a ball of dough on a work surface sprinkled with semolina. Using the heels of your hands, press down to flatten the dough. Lift and gently pull the dough to stretch it into a circle 8 inches in diameter. With your fingertips, press and shape a ½-inch rim around the crust. Repeat with remaining balls of dough.

Spread ¼ cup of the cream on each piece of dough up to the rim. Crumble the stilton over the cream and scatter the walnuts evenly on top of each pizza. Sprinkle the pizzas with the mozzarella.

Carefully slide a pizza paddle under the pizzas, one at a time, and transfer them to the oven; with a slight push, slide each pizza off the paddle onto the baking surface. Bake the pizzas for 8 to 10 minutes or until the dough is browned and crisp and the cheese is golden and bubbly.

Serves 4

BRIE AND ALMOND WITH MUSTARD SAUCE

This makes an elegant hors d'oeuvre pizza. If you like, substitute Camembert for the Brie.

4 (6-ounce) balls pizza dough; use a Standard Pizza Crust (recipe on page 14)

¾ cup crème fraîche, mascarpone, or heavy cream

¼ cup grainy Dijon-style mustard

¾ pound trimmed ripe Brie

½ cup slivered almonds

½ pound mozzarella cheese, shredded

Place a pizza brick, baking tiles, or a baking sheet in the oven and preheat the oven to 550°F.

Place a ball of dough on a work surface sprinkled with semolina. Using the heels of your hands, press down to flatten the dough. Lift and gently pull the dough to stretch it into a circle 8 inches in diameter. With your fingertips, press and shape a ½-inch rim around the crust. Repeat with remaining balls of dough.

Stir together the crème fraîche and mustard; spread one-quarter of the mixture on each piece of dough up to the rim.

Dot the Brie evenly on top of the mustard sauce. Sprinkle evenly with the almonds, then top with the mozzarella.

Carefully slide a pizza paddle under the pizzas, and transfer them to the oven; with a slight push, slide each pizza off the paddle onto the baking surface. Bake the pizzas for 8 to 10 minutes or until the dough is browned and crisp and the cheese is golden and bubbly.

Serves 4

SMOKED CHEDDAR WITH BARBECUE SAUCE

A true Western pizza.

4 (6-ounce) balls pizza
dough; use a Standard,
Sourdough, or Whole-
Wheat Pizza Crust (recipes
on pages 14–16)

1 cup Barbecue Sauce (recipe
on page 19)
6 ounces smoked cheddar
cheese, shredded
6 ounces smoked mozzarella
cheese, shredded

Place a pizza brick, baking tiles, or a baking sheet in the oven and preheat the oven to 550°F.

Place a ball of dough on a work surface sprinkled with semolina. Using the heels of your hands, press down to flatten the dough. Lift and gently pull the dough to stretch it into a circle 8 inches in diameter. With your fingertips, press and shape a ½-inch rim around the crust. Repeat with remaining balls of dough.

Spread ¼ cup of the sauce on each piece of dough up to the rim. Sprinkle the cheddar and then the mozzarella over the sauce.

Carefully slide a pizza paddle under the pizzas, one at a time, and transfer them to the oven; with a slight push, slide each pizza off the paddle onto the baking surface. Bake the pizzas for 8 to 10 minutes or until the dough is browned and crisp and the cheese is golden and bubbly.

Serves 4

SMOKED CHEESE MEDLEY WITH CREME FRAICHE

The fun of this pizza is its combination of different smoked cheeses. Use whatever combination suits your fancy.

4 (6-ounce) balls pizza
   dough; use a Standard,
   Sourdough, or Whole-
   Wheat Pizza Crust (recipes
   on pages 14–16)
1 cup crème fraîche,
   mascarpone or heavy cream

¼ pound smoked cheddar
   cheese, shredded
¼ pound smoked Gouda
   cheese, shredded
¼ pound smoked mozzarella
   cheese, shredded
¼ pound smoked Swiss
   cheese, shredded

Place a pizza brick, baking tiles, or a baking sheet in the oven and preheat the oven to 550°F.

Place a ball of dough on a work surface sprinkled with semolina. Using the heels of your hands, press down to flatten the dough. Lift and gently pull the dough to stretch it into a circle 8 inches in diameter. With your fingertips, press and shape a ½-inch rim around the crust. Repeat with remaining balls of dough.

Spread ¼ cup of the crème fraîche on each piece of dough up to the rim. Distribute all four cheeses equally among the pizzas.

Carefully slide a pizza paddle under the pizzas, one at a time, and transfer them to the oven; with a slight push, slide each pizza off the paddle onto the baking surface. Bake the pizzas for 8 to 10 minutes or until the dough is browned and crisp and the cheese is golden and bubbly.

Serves 4

FONTINA, GOAT CHEESE, PARMESAN, AND MOZZARELLA

This pizza features a perfect combination of flavors—sweet, rich fontina; tangy, creamy goat cheese; and sharp, full-flavored Parmesan. They are all blended together by the mild, slightly tangy, and sweet taste of mozzarella.

May also be made as a calzone (see page 23).

4 (6-ounce) balls pizza dough; use a Standard or Sourdough Pizza Crust (recipes on pages 14 and 16)

1 cup Tomato Sauce (recipe on page 18)

½ cup grated Parmesan cheese

¼ pound fresh creamy goat cheese

¼ pound fontina cheese

6 ounces mozzarella cheese, shredded

Place a pizza brick, baking tiles, or a baking sheet in the oven and preheat the oven to 550°F.

Place a ball of dough on a work surface sprinkled with semolina. Using the heels of your hands, press down to flatten the dough. Lift and gently pull the dough to stretch it into a circle 8 inches in diameter. With your fingertips, press and shape a ½-inch rim around the crust. Repeat with remaining balls of dough.

Spread ¼ cup of the sauce on each piece of dough up to the rim. Sprinkle the Parmesan over the sauce on each. Dot the goat cheese and fontina on top, then sprinkle evenly with the mozzarella.

Carefully slide a pizza paddle under the pizzas, one at a time, and transfer them to the oven; with a slight push, slide each pizza off the paddle onto the baking surface. Bake the pizzas for 8 to 10 minutes or until the dough is browned and crisp and the cheese is golden and bubbly.

Serves 4

INDEX

130